LUKE

MAKES SENSE OF LIFE

NEW INTERNATIONAL VERSION

Specially produced for

Billy Graham MISSION 89

HODDER AND STOUGHTON
LONDON SYDNEY AUCKLAND TORONTO

This edition of Luke's Gospel is taken from the Holy Bible, New International Version, published by Hodder and Stoughton.

British Library Cataloguing in Publication Data

[Bible. N.T. Luke. *English. New International. 1984*]
Luke: New International Version.
1. Bible. N.T. Luke—Commentaries 2. Bible
(Texts, versions, etc.)
226'.4077 BS2595.3

ISBN 0 340 51218 0

This edition first published 1984, Word List 1986, Introductory material 1989.

Printed in Great Britain for Hodder and Stoughton Limited, Mill Road, Dunton Green, Sevenoaks, Kent by Cox & Wyman Limited, Reading
Photoset by Rowland Phototypesetting Ltd, Bury St Edmunds, Suffolk
Hodder and Stoughton Editorial Office: 47 Bedford Square, London WC1B 3DP

DISCOVER THIS UNIQUE BOOK

From page 15 onwards you will be looking at one of the most famous short books ever written.

It is called 'a gospel' which simply means **good news**.

It was written over nineteen hundred years ago by a Greek doctor called Luke. During his adventurous life he met one of the most famous of the first Christians – Paul of Tarsus (St. Paul). The two became firm friends and it was from Paul that Luke learnt about Jesus of Nazareth.

As a doctor, Luke was trained to listen carefully to people and to pay attention to detail. He was soon convinced that Paul was telling the truth when he spoke about Jesus as the Son of God who had lived on earth with the special purpose of bringing people and God together.

At some stage in his life Luke travelled around Palestine to find out about Jesus from those who had been close to him. Among those he seems to have met was Mary, the mother of Jesus.

Luke's Gospel is the result of his research. He wrote it for someone called Theophilus who may well have been a Roman official that he had met on his travels. He wanted his readers to 'know the certainty of the things' that Paul and others like him taught, as the Christian message spread through the Roman Empire.

Part of the Bible

Luke's Gospel is part of the Bible – a collection of writings that the Christian churches look to as the final authority in all matters of belief.

There are two main sections in the Bible – the **Old Testament** and the **New Testament**. The Old Testament is made up of thirty-nine separate books. Some are historical, some poetic and some are written by the great prophets who spoke about God's will for the nations of Judah and Israel. All the books relate to the times before the birth of Jesus Christ and all of them were known to him.

The New Testament is made up of twenty-seven different books. There are the four Gospels, of which Luke is the third. There is a second book written by Luke called the Acts of the Apostles. This book describes the adventures of the first Christians as they reached out to the world of their day with their message about Jesus. There are also a number of letters written by leading Christians to the churches they had planted in the countries around the Mediterranean.

Finally, there is the strange but profound book known as the Revelation. This is different from all the rest and hard to understand without a wide knowledge of the issues raised in other parts of the Bible.

WHAT LUKE IS ALL ABOUT

Luke wanted his readers to become Christians. It is interesting to see how he went about trying to persuade them.

He did not mount a series of arguments for the existence of God. He did not write a string of theories. What he did was to collect and arrange a series of stories and sayings. He wanted his readers to meet Jesus for themselves. Luke had never met Jesus in the flesh, but he knew that Christianity is – more than anything else – all about that one person.

From Mary – or from those close to her – he discovered that astonishing story of the birth of Jesus. We are given a glimpse of Christ as a twelve-year-old (pages 23–24). It was obvious even then that he was someone special.

The scene shifts to Jesus as a man aged about thirty. Luke describes the events that led to him leaving his home and his work as a village carpenter. We read of the time of testing he went through in the desert (page 27). Luke was clear in his own mind that if Jesus had given in to those temptations it would have affected the whole history of the world and every one of us.

When Jesus returned to Galilee after the temptations he knew without doubt that he was truly the Son of God. Luke describes him as someone 'in the power of the Spirit' (page 28). Then Jesus begins calling people to follow him as disciples (the word means 'learners'). We read of him healing those who were sick (which interested Luke especially in the light of his experience as a doctor).

Support and Opposition

We also read of opposition. His own community in Nazareth rejected his claims to be the long-awaited person promised in the Old Testament who would make dramatic changes in the world (page 28). Soon after this Luke describes how Jesus met a more frightening sort of opposition. Evil spirits are described as affecting people and reacting violently to Jesus (page 29).

Wherever Jesus went he divided people. Some would follow him. Others would reject him. Luke knew from his research and from his own experience as a Christian that it is always like that. People are caught up in a gigantic, history-long struggle between good and evil. We cannot be neutral. We are either for Jesus or against him (page 51^{23}).

(To help you find particular parts of the Gospel it is divided into 'chapters' and 'verses'. Each verse is numbered in the text like this^{12}. In referring you to any part of the Gospel the reference will normally be given to the page and verse, for example, page 35^{37}. If more than one verse should be read then it will be set out so: page 35^{37-42}.)

Luke writes his Gospel like a modern film script. We move from one short scene to another. At one moment we see Jesus healing someone, the next we are listening-in as he teaches a few home truths to his followers. And all the time Luke is allowing his readers to see the personality of Jesus coming through.

This is important for two reasons. First, the character of Jesus is a reflection of the true character of God. Behind our existence there is an eternal fatherly God whose nature is exactly like Jesus.

Second, in the character of Jesus there is an example for us to try to copy in our daily lives.

As page follows page, however, the reader begins to sense that the opposition to Jesus is building up. Jesus makes a dramatic entry into the crowded city of Jerusalem (page 72). Many people are curious and excited as to who he is and what he is about. Others – especially the religious rulers – see him as a dangerous menace to their settled way of life. We can begin to sense that an ugly show-down may be close.

Jesus also senses that his time is short. As he gathers his followers for the traditional religious **Passover** meal (page 78) he does a strange thing. He takes some bread, breaks it and then tells his followers that his own body will be broken in death. The death, however, will not be worthless. It will, in some way, be on their behalf. "This is my body given for you," (page 79[19]).

As he pours out the wine he also likens it to the pouring out of his own blood.

Arrest and Trial

Shortly after the supper Jesus is arrested. As he is led away his followers desert him in panic.

A trial is quickly arranged. He is found guilty of blasphemy through claiming to be the Son of God (page 82[70, 71]) and a death sentence is called for. At that time Jerusalem was governed by Roman occupation forces. No death sentence could be carried out without the Governor's permission. However the Governor, Pilate, was a weak man and he finds a political storm developing over the Jesus issue. The crowds are gathering and chanting in support of a death sentence. Pilate is convinced of Christ's innocence but he breaks under the pressure and agrees to the sentence of death by crucifixion.

By page 83 we seem to be reading the ultimate tragedy. An obviously good man has been plotted against, misrepresented and put to death. Evil flourishes yet again while we join with those who look on helplessly.

Not the End

But Luke's story does not end there. On page 85 he begins to spell out an astonishing series of events that left the first followers of Jesus totally convinced that he had been brought back to life within three days of the crucifixion.

The tomb is found to be empty (page 86), but that is only the beginning. Jesus begins to appear alive to his followers (pages 87, 88). Finally, with many of his followers gathered around him Luke writes, 'While he was blessing them, he left them and was taken up into heaven' (page 88[51]). The story ends with the followers returning to Jerusalem rejoicing. They know they have lived through the greatest moments of history. They also sense that there is more to come!

Life-Changing Words

So ends Luke's historic little book, but no summary can do it justice. It has to be read and thought about. Over many centuries millions of people have read its pages and found their lives changed by its words. That is exactly what Luke wanted. He recorded on page 88 some words that Jesus said to his followers just before the final act of leaving the world:

> 'He told them, "This is what is written: The Christ will suffer and rise from the dead on the third day, and repentance and forgiveness of sins will be preached in his name to all nations, beginning at Jerusalem. You are witnesses of these things . . ."'

In writing his Gospel, Luke was trying to play a part in passing on the message that would be **good news** to people of all ages. He wanted us to discover that there really was and is a Son of God who showed his love for humanity in coming to live among us. He wanted us to see that we are all caught up in a deep battle between good and evil and that, by nature, we all tend to take sides against the pure love and goodness of God.

He wanted us also to see that the death of Jesus had, in some deep way, taken away the punishment we deserve for rejecting God. Forgiveness and a new start is on offer. We need to admit our need of that forgiveness and trust that Jesus is as real and powerful today as he was in the times of which Luke wrote.

HOW TO FIND HELP IN LUKE

The fact that you are looking through this book almost certainly means that you are thinking about the Christian faith and the whole question of Jesus.

You may, at this stage, be no more than an enquirer – someone who wants to find out more but is not yet ready to make any definite decision to become a Christian.
Section A may help you before you read further.

You may have got to the point where you are ready to become a follower of Jesus but you are not quite sure how to start.
Section B may be of help.

You may already be a Christian but you are aware of having let things slip. You want to make a fresh start. Look at section C.

You may have put your faith in Christ some time ago but you still feel unsure. Look at section D before reading further.

A. I am interested but no more than that at this stage. (Enquirer)

1 Luke would say, 'I'm glad you are interested but interest is not enough. Your eternal security depends on taking Jesus seriously and obeying him.'
Read pages 35, 36[46–49].

2 Luke would ask you to consider whether you are genuinely open to receiving what Jesus wants to say to you and your private world.
Read pages 39, 40[4–15].

3 Luke would remind you that Jesus said that a person who wanted to follow him had to realise what a big step they were taking.
Read page 45[23–26].

B. I want to become a Christian, how do I start? (Commitment)

1 Look first at the passages set out under section A.

2 Luke would point out that Jesus welcomed anyone who wanted to be his follower. Christ is on our side longing to help us. Read pages 50, 51^9–13^.

3 Read page 63^11–24^. In this famous story of the Lost Son, Jesus wanted us to see that the Father in the story was a picture of our Heavenly Father – God. Note three things in the story:

(i) The son realised he was in the wrong with his father and deliberately changed his mind about staying away from his true home. This is what **repentance** means.

(ii) The son trusted that when he got home his father would not reject him and would be able to help. He put **faith** in his father's readiness to forgive and help. He was not disappointed.

(iii) The father came running to meet his son as soon as he saw him coming. This is a picture of God's attitude to anyone who wants to start as a Christian.

4 Realise this: Jesus is near you now through his Holy Spirit. He is waiting for you to do what the Lost Son did in the story – **repent** and **believe**. Think of that story and imagine yourself as that son coming home to his father. With that picture in mind say the following prayer:

> **Father, thank you for wanting me to come home to you.**
> **I'm sorry that I have been trying to live my life far away from you.**
> **Now I have made up my mind to come to you. I want to live my life from now onwards as your son/daughter.**
> **I want you to be in charge.**
> **Thank you for the promise that you can send the Spirit of your Son Jesus into my life to help me. I ask for this to happen now.**
> **Thank you Father. Amen.**

C. I can see that I have fallen away from the faith relationship I used to have with God. I want to come back. (Rededication)

1 Read through section B.

2 Read page 81[54–62]. Peter let Jesus down badly in his hour of greatest need. We know from other parts of the New Testament that Jesus specifically forgave Peter and entrusted him with great responsibilities. The same Jesus has the same attitude to you.

3 With the picture of Peter in mind pray this prayer to the Jesus who is near.

Lord, thank you that you forgave Peter. I feel that I have been like him. I must have disappointed you. I'm sorry.
I want to start again. I want you as my Lord and my friend.
I want your Holy Spirit in my inner life to clean up what needs cleaning and to strengthen what needs strengthening.
I want your Father to be my Father.
Thank you that this can now be so. Amen.

D. I do believe but I never seem to feel very sure. (Reassurance)

1 It might be that you are the worrying type who is never too sure of anything! Many of us are like that and it can so easily affect our faith.
Read pages 54, 55[22–31]. If we put Christ first in our lives he will never let us down.

2 You may be very aware of your own failings and think that God gets tired of forgiving.
Read page 32[32] and pages 50, 51[9–13]. Remember, you have already asked God to accept you and to give you his Holy Spirit. He promises that he will do this. Stop asking and asking again and *start saying 'thank you' that God has kept his promise*!

3 You may feel unsure as to whether you will be good enough to get to heaven.
Read pages 84, 85[39–43]. The criminal dying on a cross beside Jesus had lived a wicked, unbelieving life. He had no time left to reform and make up for his past. He asked Jesus for help. Jesus promised that he would be with him after death. To be with Jesus is the same as being in heaven. *We get to heaven not because we deserve to but because Jesus wants us there and has made it possible for imperfect people to get there.*
Read page 48[20]. Jesus wants his followers to find their joy not in whether they are being 'successful' as Christians but in his promise that their names are 'written in heaven'. Say 'thank you' to God for the promise of eternal life to all who believe in him.

THE MOST FAMOUS PRAYER IN THE WORLD

They call it 'The Lord's Prayer'. It was a simple prayer that Jesus gave his followers to use as a model for all praying (page 50).

It is better known today in a longer form but the version which Luke records gives us the heart of Jesus Christ's teaching on prayer.

Read it here and think over the lessons about God and life in general which are built into those famous words.

Father,[1]
hallowed be your name,[2]
your kingdom[3] **come.**
Give us each day our daily bread.[4]
Forgive us our sins,
  for we also forgive everyone who sins against us.[5]
And lead us not into temptation.[6]

Read the prayer and look at the points set out on the next page.

[1] **Father**. The secret of knowing how to pray is knowing who is listening! Jesus taught that God is not some remote, impersonal being. God is our eternal and ultimate Father. As such he loves us and wants the best for us. He also enjoys hearing us pray and share the things that matter.

[2] The **name** of God means his reputation. The Bible solemnly warns us against taking God's name lightly. Jesus taught that we should want God to be honoured (or hallowed) in our own affairs and in the world at large. This should be the Christian's deepest concern. Jesus said that those who follow him were to make sure that 'repentance and forgiveness of sins will be preached in his name to all nations,' (page 88[47]).

[3] One of the central teachings of Jesus was that God is wanting his **kingdom** (his authority and control) to happen here in our own world. We are meant to be loyal to our own country and its laws but we have a greater loyalty to God and his laws. We are usually moved to pray when there is something we want from God. Jesus reminded us that there are also things that God wants, and these are more important. As we pray we start by telling God that we want what he wants more than we want what we want! (See page 55[31]).

[4] Once again Jesus reminds us that God is concerned about our ordinary everyday needs. To pray for our **daily bread** means to pray for the basic needs of life.

[5] **Forgiveness** is a wonderful thing! When something is forgiven it means that it is forgotten and no longer exists. No matter what our lives may have been like, when we turn to Christ and ask for forgiveness it is granted and we are considered by him to be new people. But Jesus tucked a sting in the tail of this part of the prayer. He said we should not ask God to forgive us if we are not prepared to forgive others who may do wrong things to us.

[6] These words often puzzle people. Surely God would not deliberately lead people into **temptation**? Jesus taught that God does not tempt people. This phrase, however, is meant to be a reminder to us that we are weak and need all the help we can get in dealing with temptation.

WHERE TO FIND . . .

Luke's Gospel contains some very famous passages. Here is where they may be found in this edition:

READ THROUGH LUKE IN ONE MONTH

Daily Readings

Day	Chapter and Verses	
1	1:1–38	A tale of two babies
2	1:39–80	John the Baptist is born
3	2:1–52	Jesus' early years
4	3:1–22	The voice in the desert
5	4:1–30	Temptation and rejection
6	4:31–44	Jesus the healer
7	5:1–32	The followers are called
8	5:33–6:16	The challenge to Jesus
9	6:17–49	Blessings and woes
10	7:1–35	'Are you the one who was to come . . . ?
11	7:36–8:21	Open hearts and closed minds
12	8:22–56	Jesus shows his power
13	9:1–36	Jesus – the Christ!
14	9:37–50	Conflicts
15	9:51–10:24	Sending out the followers
16	10:25–11:13	Caring and praying
17	11:14–54	Jesus and the opposition
18	12:1–59	Be prepared
19	13:1–35	The anger and sorrow of Jesus
20	14:1–35	The cost of taking sides
21	15:1–32	Finding the lost
22	16:1–31	What money cannot buy
23	17:1–37	'Whoever tries to keep his life will lose it'
24	18:1–43	Encounters with Christ
25	19:1–48	Here comes the King!
26	20:1–47	The tension mounts
27	21:1–38	The end of the age
28	22:1–71	Arrest and trial
29	23:1–56	Put to death
30	24:1–53	Alive again!

Luke

Introduction

1 Many have undertaken to draw up an account of the things
that have been fulfilled among us, [2]just as they were handed
down to us by those who from the first were eye-witnesses and
servants of the word. [3]Therefore, since I myself have carefully
investigated everything from the beginning, it seemed good also
to me to write an orderly account for you, most excellent Theophi-
lus, [4]so that you may know the certainty of the things you have
been taught.

The Birth of John the Baptist Foretold

[5]In the time of Herod king of Judea there was a priest named
Zechariah, who belonged to the priestly division of Abijah; his
wife Elizabeth was also a descendant of Aaron. [6]Both of them were
upright in the sight of God, observing all the Lord's command-
ments and regulations blamelessly. [7]But they had no children,
because Elizabeth was barren; and they were both well on in years.

[8]Once when Zechariah's division was on duty and he was
serving as priest before God, [9]he was chosen by lot, according to
the custom of the priesthood, to go into the temple of the Lord and
burn incense. [10]And when the time for the burning of incense
came, all the assembled worshippers were praying outside.

[11]Then an angel of the Lord appeared to him, standing at the
right side of the altar of incense. [12]When Zechariah saw him, he
was startled and was gripped with fear. [13]But the angel said to him:
"Do not be afraid, Zechariah; your prayer has been heard. Your
wife Elizabeth will bear you a son, and you are to give him the

An angel of the Lord appeared to him (1:11)

name John. 14He will be a joy and delight to you, and many will
rejoice because of his birth, 15for he will be great in the sight of the
Lord. He is never to take wine or other fermented drink, and he
will be filled with the Holy Spirit even from birth. 16Many of the
people of Israel will he bring back to the Lord their God. 17And he
will go on before the Lord, in the spirit and power of Elijah, to turn
the hearts of the fathers to their children and the disobedient to the
wisdom of the righteous—to make ready a people prepared for the
Lord."

18Zechariah asked the angel, "How can I be sure of this? I am an
old man and my wife is well on in years."

19The angel answered, "I am Gabriel. I stand in the presence of
God, and I have been sent to speak to you and to tell you this good
news. 20And now you will be silent and not able to speak until the
day this happens, because you did not believe my words, which
will come true at their proper time."

21Meanwhile, the people were waiting for Zechariah and
wondering why he stayed so long in the temple. 22When he came

out, he could not speak to them. They realised he had seen a vision
in the temple, for he kept making signs to them but remained
unable to speak.
23When his time of service was completed, he returned home.
24After this his wife Elizabeth became pregnant and for five
months remained in seclusion. 25"The Lord has done this for me,"
she said. "In these days he has shown his favour and taken away
my disgrace among the people."

The Birth of Jesus Foretold

26In the sixth month, God sent the angel Gabriel to Nazareth, a
town in Galilee, 27to a virgin pledged to be married to a man named
Joseph, a descendant of David. The virgin's name was Mary. 28The
angel went to her and said, "Greetings, you who are highly
favoured! The Lord is with you."
29Mary was greatly troubled at his words and wondered what
kind of greeting this might be. 30But the angel said to her, "Do not
be afraid, Mary, you have found favour with God. 31You will be
with child and give birth to a son, and you are to give him the name
Jesus. 32He will be great and will be called the Son of the Most
High. The Lord God will give him the throne of his father David,
33and he will reign over the house of Jacob for ever; his kingdom
will never end."
34"How will this be," Mary asked the angel, "since I am a
virgin?"
35The angel answered, "The Holy Spirit will come upon you,
and the power of the Most High will overshadow you. So the holy
one to be born will be called the Son of God. 36Even Elizabeth your
relative is going to have a child in her old age, and she who was
said to be barren is in her sixth month. 37For nothing is impossible
with God."
38"I am the Lord's servant," Mary answered. "May it be to me as
you have said." Then the angel left her.

Mary Visits Elizabeth

39At that time Mary got ready and hurried to a town in the hill
country of Judea, 40where she entered Zechariah's home and
greeted Elizabeth. 41When Elizabeth heard Mary's greeting, the
baby leaped in her womb, and Elizabeth was filled with the Holy
Spirit. 42In a loud voice she exclaimed: "Blessed are you among

Mary greeted Elizabeth (1:40)

women, and blessed is the child you will bear! 43But why am I so
favoured, that the mother of my Lord should come to me? 44As
soon as the sound of your greeting reached my ears, the baby in
my womb leaped for joy. 45Blessed is she who has believed that
what the Lord has said to her will be accomplished!"

Mary's Song

46And Mary said:

"My soul glorifies the Lord
47 and my spirit rejoices in God my Saviour,
48for he has been mindful
of the humble state of his servant.
From now on all generations will call me blessed,
49 for the Mighty One has done great things for me—
holy is his name.
50His mercy extends to those who fear him,
from generation to generation.
51He has performed mighty deeds with his arm;
he has scattered those who are proud in their inmost thoughts.
52He has brought down rulers from their thrones
but has lifted up the humble.

[53]He has filled the hungry with good things
but has sent the rich away empty.
[54]He has helped his servant Israel,
remembering to be merciful
[55]to Abraham and his descendants for ever,
even as he said to our fathers."

[56]Mary stayed with Elizabeth for about three months and then returned home.

The Birth of John the Baptist

[57]When it was time for Elizabeth to have her baby, she gave birth
to a son. [58]Her neighbours and relatives heard that the Lord had
shown her great mercy, and they shared her joy.
[59]On the eighth day they came to circumcise the child, and they
were going to name him after his father Zechariah, [60]but his
mother spoke up and said, "No! He is to be called John."
[61]They said to her, "There is no-one among your relatives who
has that name."
[62]Then they made signs to his father, to find out what he would
like to name the child. [63]He asked for a writing tablet, and to
everyone's astonishment he wrote, "His name is John."
[64]Immediately his mouth was opened and his tongue was loosed,
and he began to speak, praising God. [65]The neighbours were all
filled with awe, and throughout the hill country of Judea people
were talking about all these things. [66]Everyone who heard this
wondered about it, asking, "What then is this child going to be?"
For the Lord's hand was with him.

Zechariah's Song

[67]His father Zechariah was filled with the Holy Spirit and prophesied:

[68]"Praise be to the Lord, the God of Israel,
because he has come and has redeemed his people.
[69]He has raised up a hornof salvation for us
in the house of his servant David
[70](as he said through his holy prophets of long ago),
[71]salvation from our enemies
and from the hand of all who hate us—

72 to show mercy to our fathers
and to remember his holy covenant,
73 the oath he swore to our father Abraham:
74 to rescue us from the hand of our enemies,
and to enable us to serve him without fear
75 in holiness and righteousness before him all our days.

76 And you, my child, will be called a prophet of the Most High;
for you will go on before the Lord to prepare the way for him,
77 to give his people the knowledge of salvation
through the forgiveness of their sins,
78 because of the tender mercy of our God,
by which the rising sun will come to us from heaven
79 to shine on those living in darkness
and in the shadow of death,
to guide our feet into the path of peace."

80 And the child grew and became strong in spirit; and he lived in
the desert until he appeared publicly to Israel.

The Birth of Jesus

2 In those days Caesar Augustus issued a decree that a census
should be taken of the entire Roman world. (2 This was the first
census that took place while Quirinius was governor of Syria.)
3 And everyone went to his own town to register.
4 So Joseph also went up from the town of Nazareth in Galilee to
Judea, to Bethlehem the town of David, because he belonged to the
house and line of David. 5 He went there to register with Mary,
who was pledged to be married to him and was expecting a child.
6 While they were there, the time came for the baby to be born, 7 and
she gave birth to her firstborn, a son. She wrapped him in cloths
and placed him in a manger, because there was no room for them
in the inn.

The Shepherds and the Angels

8 And there were shepherds living out in the fields near by,
keeping watch over their flocks at night. 9 An angel of the Lord
appeared to them, and the glory of the Lord shone around them,
and they were terrified. 10 But the angel said to them, "Do not be
afraid. I bring you good news of great joy that will be for all the

There were shepherds, keeping watch over their flocks at night (2:8)

people. 11Today in the town of David a Saviour has been born to
you; he is Christ the Lord. 12This will be a sign to you: You will find
a baby wrapped in cloths and lying in a manger."
13Suddenly a great company of the heavenly host appeared with
the angel, praising God and saying,

14"Glory to God in the highest,
and on earth peace to men on whom his favour rests."

15When the angels had left them and gone into heaven, the
shepherds said to one another, "Let's go to Bethlehem and see this
thing that has happened, which the Lord has told us about."
16So they hurried off and found Mary and Joseph, and the baby,
who was lying in the manger. 17When they had seen him, they
spread the word concerning what had been told them about this
child, 18and all who heard it were amazed at what the shepherds
said to them. 19But Mary treasured up all these things and pon-
dered them in her heart. 20The shepherds returned, glorifying and

praising God for all the things they had heard and seen, which were just as they had been told.

Jesus Presented in the Temple

21On the eighth day, when it was time to circumcise him, he was
named Jesus, the name the angel had given him before he had
been conceived.
22When the time of their purification according to the Law of
Moses had been completed, Joseph and Mary took him to Jeru-
salem to present him to the Lord 23(as it is written in the Law of the
Lord, "Every firstborn male is to be consecrated to the Lord"),
24and to offer a sacrifice in keeping with what is said in the Law of
the Lord: "a pair of doves or two young pigeons".
25Now there was a man in Jerusalem called Simeon, who was
righteous and devout. He was waiting for the consolation of Israel,
and the Holy Spirit was upon him. 26It had been revealed to him by
the Holy Spirit that he would not die before he had seen the Lord's
Christ. 27Moved by the Spirit, he went into the temple courts.
When the parents brought in the child Jesus to do for him what the
custom of the Law required, 28Simeon took him in his arms and
praised God, saying:

29"Sovereign Lord, as you have promised,
    you now dismiss your servant in peace.
30For my eyes have seen your salvation,
31   which you have prepared in the sight of all people,
32a light for revelation to the Gentiles
    and for glory to your people Israel."

33The child's father and mother marvelled at what was said
about him. 34Then Simeon blessed them and said to Mary, his
mother: "This child is destined to cause the falling and rising of
many in Israel, and to be a sign that will be spoken against, 35so
that the thoughts of many hearts will be revealed. And a sword
will pierce your own soul too."
36There was also a prophetess, Anna, the daughter of Phanuel,
of the tribe of Asher. She was very old; she had lived with her
husband seven years after her marriage, 37and then was a widow
until she was eighty-four. She never left the temple but wor-
shipped night and day, fasting and praying. 38Coming up to them
at that very moment, she gave thanks to God and spoke about the

Simeon took him in his arms and praised God (2:28)

child to all who were looking forward to the redemption of Jerusalem.
[39]When Joseph and Mary had done everything required by the
Law of the Lord, they returned to Galilee to their own town of
Nazareth. [40]And the child grew and became strong; he was filled
with wisdom, and the grace of God was upon him.

The Boy Jesus at the Temple

[41]Every year his parents went to Jerusalem for the Feast of the
Passover. [42]When he was twelve years old, they went up to the
Feast, according to the custom. [43]After the Feast was over, while
his parents were returning home, the boy Jesus stayed behind in
Jerusalem, but they were unaware of it. [44]Thinking he was in their
company, they travelled on for a day. Then they began looking for
him among their relatives and friends. [45]When they did not find
him, they went back to Jerusalem to look for him. [46]After three
days they found him in the temple courts, sitting among the
teachers, listening to them and asking them questions. [47]Everyone
who heard him was amazed at his understanding and his answers.
[48]When his parents saw him, they were astonished. His mother
said to him, "Son, why have you treated us like this? Your father
and I have been anxiously searching for you."
[49]"Why were you searching for me?" he asked. "Didn't you

know I had to be in my Father's house?" 50But they did not
understand what he was saying to them.
51Then he went down to Nazareth with them and was obedient
to them. But his mother treasured all these things in her heart.
52And Jesus grew in wisdom and stature, and in favour with God
and men.

John the Baptist Prepares the Way

3 In the fifteenth year of the reign of Tiberius Caesar—when
Pontius Pilate was governor of Judea, Herod tetrarch of
Galilee, his brother Philip tetrarch of Iturea and Traconitis, and
Lysanias tetrarch of Abilene—2during the high priesthood of
Annas and Caiaphas, the word of God came to John son of
Zechariah in the desert. 3He went into all the country around the
Jordan, preaching a baptism of repentance for the forgiveness of
sins. 4As is written in the book of the words of Isaiah the prophet:

"A voice of one calling in the desert,
'Prepare the way for the Lord,
  make straight paths for him.
5Every valley shall be filled in,
  every mountain and hill made low.
The crooked roads shall become straight,
  the rough ways smooth.
6And all mankind will see God's salvation.' "

7John said to the crowds coming out to be baptised by him, "You
brood of vipers! Who warned you to flee from the coming wrath?
8Produce fruit in keeping with repentance. And do not begin to say
to yourselves, 'We have Abraham as our father.' For I tell you that
out of these stones God can raise up children for Abraham. 9The
axe is already at the root of the trees, and every tree that does not
produce good fruit will be cut down and thrown into the fire."
10"What should we do then?" the crowd asked.
11John answered, "The man with two tunics should share with
him who has none, and the one who has food should do the
same."
12Tax collectors also came to be baptised. "Teacher," they asked,
"what should we do?"
13"Don't collect any more than you are required to," he told
them.

14 Then some soldiers asked him, "And what should we do?"
He replied, "Don't extort money and don't accuse people falsely
—be content with your pay."
15 The people were waiting expectantly and were all wondering
in their hearts if John might possibly be the Christ. 16 John answered
them all, "I baptise you with water. But one more powerful than I
will come, the thongs of whose sandals I am not worthy to untie.
He will baptise you with the Holy Spirit and with fire. 17 His
winnowing fork is in his hand to clear his threshing-floor and to
gather the wheat into his barn, but he will burn up the chaff with
unquenchable fire." 18 And with many other words John exhorted
the people and preached the good news to them.
19 But when John rebuked Herod the tetrarch because of Hero-
dias, his brother's wife, and all the other evil things he had done,
20 Herod added this to them all: He locked John up in prison.

The Baptism and Genealogy of Jesus

21 When all the people were being baptised, Jesus was baptised
too. And as he was praying, heaven was opened 22 and the Holy
Spirit descended on him in bodily form like a dove. And a voice
came from heaven: "You are my Son, whom I love; with you I am
well pleased."

The Holy Spirit descended like a dove (3:22)

23Now Jesus himself was about thirty years old when he began his ministry. He was the son, so it was thought, of Joseph,

the son of Heli, 24the son of Matthat,
the son of Levi, the son of Melki,
the son of Jannai, the son of Joseph,
25the son of Mattathias, the son of Amos,
the son of Nahum, the son of Esli,
the son of Naggai, 26the son of Maath,
the son of Mattathias, the son of Semein,
the son of Josech, the son of Joda,
27the son of Joanan, the son of Rhesa,
the son of Zerubbabel, the son of Shealtiel,
the son of Neri, 28the son of Melki,
the son of Addi, the son of Cosam,
the son of Elmadam, the son of Er,
29the son of Joshua, the son of Eliezer,
the son of Jorim, the son of Matthat,
the son of Levi, 30the son of Simeon,
the son of Judah, the son of Joseph,
the son of Jonam, the son of Eliakim,
31the son of Melea, the son of Menna,
the son of Mattatha, the son of Nathan,
the son of David, 32the son of Jesse,
the son of Obed, the son of Boaz,
the son of Salmon, the son of Nahshon,
33the son of Amminadab, the son of Ram,
the son of Hezron, the son of Perez,
the son of Judah, 34the son of Jacob,
the son of Isaac, the son of Abraham,
the son of Terah, the son of Nahor,
35the son of Serug, the son of Reu,
the son of Peleg, the son of Eber,
the son of Shelah, 36the son of Cainan,
the son of Arphaxad, the son of Shem,
the son of Noah, the son of Lamech,
37the son of Methuselah, the son of Enoch,
the son of Jared, the son of Mahalalel,
the son of Kenan, 38the son of Enosh,
the son of Seth, the son of Adam,
the son of God.

The Temptation of Jesus

4 Jesus, full of the Holy Spirit, returned from the Jordan and
was led by the Spirit in the desert, 2where for forty days he
was tempted by the devil. He ate nothing during those days, and
at the end of them he was hungry.
3The devil said to him, "If you are the Son of God, tell this stone
to become bread."
4Jesus answered, "It is written: 'Man does not live on bread
alone.'"

Man does not live on bread alone (4:4)

5The devil led him up to a high place and showed him in an
instant all the kingdoms of the world. 6And he said to him, "I will
give you all their authority and splendour, for it has been given to
me, and I can give it to anyone I want to. 7So if you worship me, it
will all be yours."
8Jesus answered, "It is written: 'Worship the Lord your God and
serve him only.'"
9The devil led him to Jerusalem and had him stand on the

highest point of the temple. "If you are the Son of God," he said,
"throw yourself down from here. [10]For it is written:

"'He will command his angels concerning you
to guard you carefully;
[11]they will lift you up in their hands,
so that you will not strike your foot against a stone.'"

[12]Jesus answered, "It says: 'Do not put the Lord your God to the
test.'"
[13]When the devil had finished all this tempting, he left him until
an opportune time.

Jesus Rejected at Nazareth

[14]Jesus returned to Galilee in the power of the Spirit, and news
about him spread through the whole countryside. [15]He taught in
their synagogues, and everyone praised him.
[16]He went to Nazareth, where he had been brought up, and on
the Sabbath day he went into the synagogue, as was his custom.
And he stood up to read. [17]The scroll of the prophet Isaiah was
handed to him. Unrolling it, he found the place where it is written:

[18]"The Spirit of the Lord is on me,
because he has anointed me
to preach good news to the poor.
He has sent me to proclaim freedom for the prisoners
and recovery of sight for the blind,
to release the oppressed,
[19] to proclaim the year of the Lord's favour."

[20]Then he rolled up the scroll, gave it back to the attendant and
sat down. The eyes of everyone in the synagogue were fastened on
him, [21]and he began by saying to them, "Today this scripture is
fulfilled in your hearing."
[22]All spoke well of him and were amazed at the gracious words
that came from his lips. "Isn't this Joseph's son?" they asked.
[23]Jesus said to them, "Surely you will quote this proverb to me:
'Physician, heal yourself! Do here in your home town what we
have heard that you did in Capernaum.'"
[24]"I tell you the truth," he continued, "no prophet is accepted in
his home town. [25]I assure you that there were many widows in

Israel in Elijah's time, when the sky was shut for three and a half
years and there was a severe famine throughout the land. 26 Yet
Elijah was not sent to any of them, but to a widow in Zarephath in
the region of Sidon. 27 And there were many in Israel with leprosy
in the time of Elisha the prophet, yet not one of them was
cleansed—only Naaman the Syrian."
28 All the people in the synagogue were furious when they heard
this. 29 They got up, drove him out of the town, and took him to the
brow of the hill on which the town was built, in order to throw him
down the cliff. 30 But he walked right through the crowd and went
on his way.

Jesus Drives Out an Evil Spirit

31 Then he went down to Capernaum, a town in Galilee, and on
the Sabbath began to teach the people. 32 They were amazed at his
teaching, because his message had authority.
33 In the synagogue there was a man possessed by a demon, an
evil spirit. He cried out at the top of his voice, 34 "Ha! What do you
want with us, Jesus of Nazareth? Have you come to destroy us? I
know who you are—the Holy One of God!"
35 "Be quiet!" Jesus said sternly. "Come out of him!" Then the
demon threw the man down before them all and came out without
injuring him.
36 All the people were amazed and said to each other, "What is
this teaching? With authority and power he gives orders to evil
spirits and they come out!" 37 And the news about him spread
throughout the surrounding area.

Jesus Heals Many

38 Jesus left the synagogue and went to the home of Simon. Now
Simon's mother-in-law was suffering from a high fever, and they
asked Jesus to help her. 39 So he bent over her and rebuked the
fever, and it left her. She got up at once and began to wait on them.
40 When the sun was setting, the people brought to Jesus all who
had various kinds of sickness, and laying his hands on each one,
he healed them. 41 Moreover, demons came out of many people,
shouting, "You are the Son of God!" But he rebuked them and
would not allow them to speak, because they knew he was the
Christ.
42 At daybreak Jesus went out to a solitary place. The people were

looking for him and when they came to where he was, they tried to
keep him from leaving them. [43]But he said, "I must preach the
good news of the kingdom of God to the other towns also, because
that is why I was sent." [44]And he kept on preaching in the
synagogues of Judea.

The Calling of the First Disciples

5 One day as Jesus was standing by the Lake of Gennesaret,
with the people crowding round him and listening to the
word of God, [2]he saw at the water's edge two boats, left there by
the fishermen, who were washing their nets. [3]He got into one of
the boats, the one belonging to Simon, and asked him to put out a
little from shore. Then he sat down and taught the people from the
boat.

[4]When he had finished speaking, he said to Simon, "Put out into
deep water, and let down the nets for a catch."

[5]Simon answered, "Master, we've worked hard all night and
haven't caught anything. But because you say so, I will let down
the nets."

[6]When they had done so, they caught such a large number of
fish that their nets began to break. [7]So they signalled to their
partners in the other boat to come and help them, and they came
and filled both boats so full that they began to sink.

[8]When Simon Peter saw this, he fell at Jesus' knees and said,
"Go away from me, Lord; I am a sinful man!" [9]For he and all his
companions were astonished at the catch of fish they had taken,
[10]and so were James and John, the sons of Zebedee, Simon's
partners.

Then Jesus said to Simon, "Don't be afraid; from now on you
will catch men." [11]So they pulled their boats up on shore, left
everything and followed him.

The Man With Leprosy

[12]While Jesus was in one of the towns, a man came along who
was covered with leprosy. When he saw Jesus, he fell with his face
to the ground and begged him, "Lord, if you are willing, you can
make me clean."

[13]Jesus reached out his hand and touched the man. "I am
willing," he said. "Be clean!" And immediately the leprosy left
him.

[14]Then Jesus ordered him, "Don't tell anyone, but go, show yourself to the priest and offer the sacrifices that Moses commanded for your cleansing, as a testimony to them."

[15]Yet the news about him spread all the more, so that crowds of people came to hear him and to be healed of their sicknesses. [16]But Jesus often withdrew to lonely places and prayed.

Jesus Heals a Paralytic

[17]One day as he was teaching, Pharisees and teachers of the law, who had come from every village of Galilee and from Judea and Jerusalem, were sitting there. And the power of the Lord was present for him to heal the sick. [18]Some men came carrying a paralytic on a mat and tried to take him into the house to lay him before Jesus. [19]When they could not find a way to do this because of the crowd, they went up on the roof and lowered him on his mat through the tiles into the middle of the crowd, right in front of Jesus.

[20]When Jesus saw their faith, he said, "Friend, your sins are forgiven."

[21]The Pharisees and the teachers of the law began thinking to themselves, "Who is this fellow who speaks blasphemy? Who can forgive sins but God alone?"

[22]Jesus knew what they were thinking and asked, "Why are you thinking these things in your hearts? [23]Which is easier: to say, 'Your sins are forgiven,' or to say, 'Get up and walk'? [24]But that you may know that the Son of Man has authority on earth to forgive sins. . . ." He said to the paralysed man, "I tell you, get up, take your mat and go home." [25]Immediately he stood up in front of them, took what he had been lying on and went home praising God. [26]Everyone was amazed and gave praise to God. They were filled with awe and said, "We have seen remarkable things today."

The Calling of Levi

[27]After this, Jesus went out and saw a tax collector by the name of Levi sitting at his tax booth. "Follow me," Jesus said to him, [28]and Levi got up, left everything and followed him.

[29]Then Levi held a great banquet for Jesus at his house, and a large crowd of tax collectors and others were eating with them. [30]But the Pharisees and the teachers of the law who belonged to their sect complained to his disciples, "Why do you eat and drink

with tax collectors and 'sinners'?"
31 Jesus answered them, "It is not the healthy who need a doctor,
but the sick. 32 I have not come to call the righteous, but sinners to
repentance."

Jesus Questioned About Fasting

33 They said to him, "John's disciples often fast and pray, and so
do the disciples of the Pharisees, but yours go on eating and
drinking."
34 Jesus answered, "Can you make the guests of the bridegroom
fast while he is with them? 35 But the time will come when the
bridegroom will be taken from them; in those days they will fast."
36 He told them this parable: "No-one tears a patch from a new
garment and sews it on an old one. If he does, he will have torn the
new garment, and the patch from the new will not match the old.
37 And no-one pours new wine into old wineskins. If he does, the
new wine will burst the skins, the wine will run out and the
wineskins will be ruined. 38 No, new wine must be poured into new
wineskins. 39 And no-one after drinking old wine wants the new,
for he says, 'The old is better.'"

Lord of the Sabbath

6 One Sabbath Jesus was going through the cornfields, and his
disciples began to pick some ears of corn, rub them in their
hands and eat the grain. 2 Some of the Pharisees asked, "Why are
you doing what is unlawful on the Sabbath?"
3 Jesus answered them, "Have you never read what David did
when he and his companions were hungry? 4 He entered the house
of God, and taking the consecrated bread, he ate what is lawful
only for priests to eat. And he also gave some to his companions."
5 Then Jesus said to them, "The Son of Man is Lord of the Sabbath."
6 On another Sabbath he went into the synagogue and was
teaching, and a man was there whose right hand was shrivelled.
7 The Pharisees and the teachers of the law were looking for a
reason to accuse Jesus, so they watched him closely to see if he
would heal on the Sabbath. 8 But Jesus knew what they were
thinking and said to the man with the shrivelled hand, "Get up
and stand in front of everyone." So he got up and stood there.
9 Then Jesus said to them, "I ask you, which is lawful on the
Sabbath: to do good or to do evil, to save life or to destroy it?"

Jesus was going through the cornfields (6:1)

10He looked round at them all, and then said to the man, "Stretch out your hand." He did so, and his hand was completely restored. 11But they were furious and began to discuss with one another what they might do to Jesus.

The Twelve Apostles

12One of those days Jesus went out to a mountainside to pray,
and spent the night praying to God. 13When morning came, he
called his disciples to him and chose twelve of them, whom he also
designated apostles: 14Simon (whom he named Peter), his brother
Andrew, James, John, Philip, Bartholomew, 15Matthew, Thomas,
James son of Alphaeus, Simon who was called the Zealot, 16Judas
son of James, and Judas Iscariot, who became a traitor.

Blessings and Woes

[17]He went down with them and stood on a level place. A large
crowd of his disciples was there and a great number of people from
all over Judea, from Jerusalem, and from the coast of Tyre and
Sidon, [18]who had come to hear him and to be healed of their
diseases. Those troubled by evil spirits were cured, [19]and the
people all tried to touch him, because power was coming from him
and healing them all.

[20]Looking at his disciples, he said:

"Blessed are you who are poor,
for yours is the kingdom of God.
[21]Blessed are you who hunger now,
for you will be satisfied.
Blessed are you who weep now,
for you will laugh.
[22]Blessed are you when men hate you,
when they exclude you and insult you
and reject your name as evil,
because of the Son of Man.

[23]"Rejoice in that day and leap for joy, because great is your reward in heaven. For that is how their fathers treated the prophets.

[24]"But woe to you who are rich,
for you have already received your comfort.
[25]Woe to you who are well fed now,
for you will go hungry.
Woe to you who laugh now,
for you will mourn and weep.
[26]Woe to you when all men speak well of you,
for that is how their fathers treated the false prophets.

Love for Enemies

[27]"But I tell you who hear me: Love your enemies, do good to
those who hate you, [28]bless those who curse you, pray for those
who ill-treat you. [29]If someone strikes you on one cheek, turn to
him the other also. If someone takes your cloak, do not stop him
from taking your tunic. [30]Give to everyone who asks you, and if

anyone takes what belongs to you, do not demand it back. 31Do to others as you would have them do to you.

32"If you love those who love you, what credit is that to you? Even 'sinners' love those who love them. 33And if you do good to those who are good to you, what credit is that to you? Even 'sinners' do that. 34And if you lend to those from whom you expect repayment, what credit is that to you? Even 'sinners' lend to 'sinners', expecting to be repaid in full. 35But love your enemies, do good to them, and lend to them without expecting to get anything back. Then your reward will be great, and you will be sons of the Most High, because he is kind to the ungrateful and wicked. 36Be merciful, just as your Father is merciful.

Judging Others

37"Do not judge, and you will not be judged. Do not condemn, and you will not be condemned. Forgive, and you will be forgiven. 38Give, and it will be given to you. A good measure, pressed down, shaken together and running over, will be poured into your lap. For with the measure you use, it will be measured to you."

39He also told them this parable: "Can a blind man lead a blind man? Will they not both fall into a pit? 40A student is not above his teacher, but everyone who is fully trained will be like his teacher.

41"Why do you look at the speck of sawdust in your brother's eye and pay no attention to the plank in your own eye? 42How can you say to your brother, 'Brother, let me take the speck out of your eye,' when you yourself fail to see the plank in your own eye? You hypocrite, first take the plank out of your eye, and then you will see clearly to remove the speck from your brother's eye.

A Tree and Its Fruit

43"No good tree bears bad fruit, nor does a bad tree bear good fruit. 44Each tree is recognised by its own fruit. People do not pick figs from thornbushes, or grapes from briers. 45The good man brings good things out of the good stored up in his heart, and the evil man brings evil things out of the evil stored up in his heart. For out of the overflow of his heart his mouth speaks.

The Wise and Foolish Builders

46"Why do you call me, 'Lord, Lord,' and do not do what I say?

47I will show you what he is like who comes to me and hears my
words and puts them into practice. 48He is like a man building a
house, who dug down deep and laid the foundation on rock.
When the flood came, the torrent struck that house but could not
shake it, because it was well built. 49But the one who hears my
words and does not put them into practice is like a man who built a
house on the ground without a foundation. The moment the
torrent struck that house, it collapsed and its destruction was
complete."

The Faith of the Centurion

7 When Jesus had finished saying all this in the hearing of the
people, he entered Capernaum. 2There a centurion's servant,
whom his master valued highly, was sick and about to die. 3The
centurion heard of Jesus and sent some elders of the Jews to him,
asking him to come and heal his servant. 4When they came to
Jesus, they pleaded earnestly with him, "This man deserves to
have you do this, 5because he loves our nation and has built our
synagogue." 6So Jesus went with them.
He was not far from the house when the centurion sent friends
to say to him: "Lord, don't trouble yourself, for I do not deserve to
have you come under my roof. 7That is why I did not even consider
myself worthy to come to you. But say the word, and my servant
will be healed. 8For I myself am a man under authority, with
soldiers under me. I tell this one, 'Go', and he goes; and that one,
'Come', and he comes. I say to my servant, 'Do this', and he does
it."
9When Jesus heard this, he was amazed at him, and turning to
the crowd following him, he said, "I tell you, I have not found such
great faith even in Israel." 10Then the men who had been sent
returned to the house and found the servant well.

Jesus Raises a Widow's Son

11Soon afterwards, Jesus went to a town called Nain, and his
disciples and a large crowd went along with him. 12As he
approached the town gate, a dead person was being carried
out—the only son of his mother, and she was a widow. And a
large crowd from the town was with her. 13When the Lord saw her,
his heart went out to her and he said, "Don't cry."
14Then he went up and touched the coffin, and those carrying it

stood still. He said, "Young man, I say to you, get up!" 15The dead
man sat up and began to talk, and Jesus gave him back to his
mother.
16They were all filled with awe and praised God. "A great
prophet has appeared among us," they said. "God has come to
help his people." 17This news about Jesus spread throughout Judea
and the surrounding country.

Jesus and John the Baptist

18John's disciples told him about all these things. Calling two of
them, 19he sent them to the Lord to ask, "Are you the one who was
to come, or should we expect someone else?"
20When the men came to Jesus, they said, "John the Baptist sent
us to you to ask, 'Are you the one who was to come, or should we
expect someone else?'"
21At that very time Jesus cured many who had diseases, sick-
nesses and evil spirits, and gave sight to many who were blind.
22So he replied to the messengers, "Go back and report to John
what you have seen and heard: The blind receive sight, the lame
walk, those who have leprosy are cured, the deaf hear, the dead
are raised, and the good news is preached to the poor. 23Blessed is
the man who does not fall away on account of me."
24After John's messengers left, Jesus began to speak to the crowd
about John: "What did you go out into the desert to see? A reed
swayed by the wind? 25If not, what did you go out to see? A man
dressed in fine clothes? No, those who wear expensive clothes and
indulge in luxury are in palaces. 26But what did you go out to see?
A prophet? Yes, I tell you, and more than a prophet. 27This is the
one about whom it is written:

"'I will send my messenger ahead of you,
who will prepare your way before you.'

28I tell you, among those born of women there is no-one greater
than John; yet the one who is least in the kingdom of God is greater
than he."
(29All the people, even the tax collectors, when they heard Jesus'
words, acknowledged that God's way was right, because they had
been baptised by John. 30But the Pharisees and experts in the law
rejected God's purpose for themselves, because they had not been
baptised by John.)

31"To what, then, can I compare the people of this generation?
What are they like? 32They are like children sitting in the market-
place and calling out to each other:

" 'We played the flute for you,
and you did not dance;
we sang a dirge,
and you did not cry.'

33For John the Baptist came neither eating bread nor drinking
wine, and you say, 'He has a demon.' 34The Son of Man came
eating and drinking, and you say, 'Here is a glutton and a drunk-
ard, a friend of tax collectors and "sinners".' 35But wisdom is
proved right by all her children."

Jesus Anointed by a Sinful Woman

36Now one of the Pharisees invited Jesus to have dinner with
him, so he went to the Pharisee's house and reclined at the table.
37When a woman who had lived a sinful life in that town learned
that Jesus was eating at the Pharisee's house, she brought an
alabaster jar of perfume, 38and as she stood behind him at his feet
weeping, she began to wet his feet with her tears. Then she wiped
them with her hair, kissed them and poured perfume on them.
39When the Pharisee who had invited him saw this, he said to
himself, "If this man were a prophet, he would know who is
touching him and what kind of woman she is—that she is a
sinner."
40Jesus answered him, "Simon, I have something to tell you."
"Tell me, teacher," he said.
41"Two men owed money to a certain money-lender. One owed
him five hundred denarii, and the other fifty. 42Neither of them
had the money to pay him back, so he cancelled the debts of both.
Now which of them will love him more?"
43Simon replied, "I suppose the one who had the bigger debt
cancelled."
"You have judged correctly," Jesus said.
44Then he turned towards the woman and said to Simon, "Do
you see this woman? I came into your house. You did not give me
any water for my feet, but she wet my feet with her tears and
wiped them with her hair. 45You did not give me a kiss, but this

woman, from the time I entered has not stopped kissing my feet. [46]You did not put oil on my head, but she has poured perfume on my feet. [47]Therefore, I tell you, her many sins have been forgiven—for she loved much. But he who has been forgiven little loves little."

[48]Then Jesus said to her, "Your sins are forgiven."

[49]The other guests began to say among themselves, "Who is this who even forgives sins?"

[50]Jesus said to the woman, "Your faith has saved you; go in peace."

The Parable of the Sower

8 After this, Jesus travelled about from one town and village to another, proclaiming the good news of the kingdom of God. The Twelve were with him, [2]and also some women who had been cured of evil spirits and diseases: Mary (called Magdalene) from whom seven demons had come out; [3]Joanna the wife of Chuza, the manager of Herod's household; Susanna; and many others. These women were helping to support them out of their own means.

[4]While a large crowd was gathering and people were coming to Jesus from town after town, he told this parable: [5]"A farmer went out to sow his seed. As he was scattering the seed, some fell along the path; it was trampled on, and the birds of the air ate it up. [6]Some fell on rock, and when it came up, the plants withered because they had no moisture. [7]Other seed fell among thorns, which grew up with it and choked the plants. [8]Still other seed fell on good soil. It came up and yielded a crop, a hundred times more than was sown."

When he said this, he called out, "He who has ears to hear, let him hear."

[9]His disciples asked him what this parable meant. [10]He said, "The knowledge of the secrets of the kingdom of God has been given to you, but to others I speak in parables, so that,

"'though seeing, they may not see;
though hearing, they may not understand.'

[11]"This is the meaning of the parable: The seed is the word of God. [12]Those along the path are the ones who hear, and then the devil comes and takes away the word from their hearts, so that

they may not believe and be saved. 13Those on the rock are the
ones who receive the word with joy when they hear it, but they
have no root. They believe for a while, but in the time of testing
they fall away. 14The seed that fell among thorns stands for those
who hear, but as they go on their way they are choked by life's
worries, riches and pleasures, and they do not mature. 15But the
seed on good soil stands for those with a noble and good heart,
who hear the word, retain it, and by persevering produce a crop.

A Lamp on a Stand

16"No-one lights a lamp and hides it in a jar or puts it under a
bed. Instead, he puts it on a stand, so that those who come in can
see the light. 17For there is nothing hidden that will not be
disclosed, and nothing concealed that will not be known or
brought out into the open. 18Therefore consider carefully how you
listen. Whoever has will be given more; whoever does not have,
even what he thinks he has will be taken from him."

Jesus' Mother and Brothers

19Now Jesus' mother and brothers came to see him, but they
were not able to get near him because of the crowd. 20Someone told
him, "Your mother and brothers are standing outside, wanting to
see you."

21He replied, "My mother and brothers are those who hear
God's word and put it into practice."

Jesus Calms the Storm

22One day Jesus said to his disciples, "Let's go over to the other
side of the lake." So they got into a boat and set out. 23As they
sailed, he fell asleep. A squall came down on the lake, so that the
boat was being swamped, and they were in great danger.

24The disciples went and woke him, saying, "Master, Master,
we're going to drown!"

He got up and rebuked the wind and the raging waters; the
storm subsided, and all was calm. 25"Where is your faith?" he
asked his disciples.

In fear and amazement they asked one another, "Who is this?
He commands even the winds and the water, and they obey him."

A squall came down on the lake (8:23)

The Healing of a Demon-possessed Man

[26]They sailed to the region of the Gerasenes, which is across the lake from Galilee. [27]When Jesus stepped ashore, he was met by a demon-possessed man from the town. For a long time this man had not worn clothes or lived in a house, but had lived in the tombs. [28]When he saw Jesus, he cried out and fell at his feet, shouting at the top of his voice, "What do you want with me, Jesus, Son of the Most High God? I beg you, don't torture me!" [29]For Jesus had commanded the evil spirit to come out of the man. Many times it had seized him, and though he was chained hand and foot and kept under guard, he had broken his chains and had been driven by the demon into solitary places.

[30]Jesus asked him, "What is your name?"

"Legion," he replied, because many demons had gone into him.

31 And they begged him repeatedly not to order them to go into the
Abyss.
32 A large herd of pigs was feeding there on the hillside. The
demons begged Jesus to let them go into them, and he gave them
permission. 33 When the demons came out of the man, they went
into the pigs, and the herd rushed down the steep bank into the
lake and was drowned.
34 When those tending the pigs saw what had happened, they
ran off and reported this in the town and countryside, 35 and the
people went out to see what had happened. When they came to
Jesus, they found the man from whom the demons had gone out,
sitting at Jesus' feet, dressed and in his right mind; and they were
afraid. 36 Those who had seen it told the people how the demon-
possessed man had been cured. 37 Then all the people of the region
of the Gerasenes asked Jesus to leave them, because they were
overcome with fear. So he got into the boat and left.
38 The man from whom the demons had gone out begged to go
with him, but Jesus sent him away, saying, 39 "Return home and
tell how much God has done for you." So the man went away and
told all over the town how much Jesus had done for him.

A Dead Girl and a Sick Woman

40 Now when Jesus returned, a crowd welcomed him, for they
were all expecting him. 41 Then a man named Jairus, a ruler of the
synagogue, came and fell at Jesus' feet, pleading with him to come
to his house 42 because his only daughter, a girl of about twelve,
was dying.
As Jesus was on his way, the crowds almost crushed him. 43 And
a woman was there who had been subject to bleeding for twelve
years, but no-one could heal her. 44 She came up behind him and
touched the edge of his cloak, and immediately her bleeding
stopped.
45 "Who touched me?" Jesus asked.
When they all denied it, Peter said, "Master, the people are
crowding and pressing against you."
46 But Jesus said, "Someone touched me; I know that power has
gone out from me."
47 Then the woman, seeing that she could not go unnoticed,
came trembling and fell at his feet. In the presence of all the people,
she told why she had touched him and how she had been instantly

healed. 48Then he said to her, "Daughter, your faith has healed you. Go in peace."

49While Jesus was still speaking, someone came from the house of Jairus, the synagogue ruler. "Your daughter is dead," he said. "Don't bother the teacher any more."

50Hearing this, Jesus said to Jairus, "Don't be afraid; just believe, and she will be healed."

51When he arrived at the house of Jairus, he did not let anyone go in with him except Peter, John and James, and the child's father and mother. 52Meanwhile, all the people were wailing and mourning for her. "Stop wailing," Jesus said. "She is not dead but asleep."

53They laughed at him, knowing that she was dead. 54But he took her by the hand and said, "My child, get up!" 55Her spirit returned, and at once she stood up. Then Jesus told them to give her something to eat. 56Her parents were astonished, but he ordered them not to tell anyone what had happened.

Jesus Sends Out the Twelve

9 When Jesus had called the Twelve together, he gave them power and authority to drive out all demons and to cure diseases, 2and he sent them out to preach the kingdom of God and to heal the sick. 3He told them: "Take nothing for the journey—no staff, no bag, no bread, no money, no extra tunic. 4Whatever house you enter, stay there until you leave that town. 5If people do not welcome you, shake the dust off your feet when you leave their town, as a testimony against them." 6So they set out and went from village to village, preaching the gospel and healing people everywhere.

7Now Herod the tetrarch heard about all that was going on. And he was perplexed, because some were saying that John had been raised from the dead, 8others that Elijah had appeared, and still others that one of the prophets of long ago had come back to life. 9But Herod said, "I beheaded John. Who, then, is this I hear such things about?" And he tried to see him.

Jesus Feeds the Five Thousand

10When the apostles returned, they reported to Jesus what they had done. Then he took them with him and they withdrew by themselves to a town called Bethsaida, 11but the crowds learned

about it and followed him. He welcomed them and spoke to them about the kingdom of God, and healed those who needed healing.
12 Late in the afternoon the Twelve came to him and said, "Send the crowd away so they can go to the surrounding villages and countryside and find food and lodging, because we are in a remote place here."
13 He replied, "You give them something to eat."

They answered, "We have only five loaves of bread and two fish—unless we go and buy food for all this crowd."
14 (About five thousand men were there.)

But he said to his disciples, "Make them sit down in groups of about fifty each."
15 The disciples did so, and everybody sat down.
16 Taking the five loaves and the two fish and looking up to heaven, he gave thanks and broke them. Then he gave them to the disciples to set before the people.
17 They all ate and were satisfied, and the disciples picked up twelve basketfuls of broken pieces that were left over.

They all ate and were satisfied (9:17)

Peter's Confession of Christ

[18]Once when Jesus was praying in private and his disciples were with him, he asked them, "Who do the crowds say I am?"

[19]They replied, "Some say John the Baptist; others say Elijah; and still others, that one of the prophets of long ago has come back to life."

[20]"But what about you?" he asked. "Who do you say I am?"

Peter answered, "The Christ of God."

[21]Jesus strictly warned them not to tell this to anyone. [22]And he said, "The Son of Man must suffer many things and be rejected by the elders, chief priests and teachers of the law, and he must be killed and on the third day be raised to life."

[23]Then he said to them all: "If anyone would come after me, he must deny himself and take up his cross daily and follow me. [24]For whoever wants to save his life will lose it, but whoever loses his life for me will save it. [25]What good is it for a man to gain the whole world, and yet lose or forfeit his very self? [26]If anyone is ashamed of me and my words, the Son of Man will be ashamed of him when he comes in his glory and in the glory of the Father and of the holy angels. [27]I tell you the truth, some who are standing here will not taste death before they see the kingdom of God."

The Transfiguration

[28]About eight days after Jesus said this, he took Peter, John and James with him and went up onto a mountain to pray. [29]As he was praying, the appearance of his face changed, and his clothes became as bright as a flash of lightning. [30]Two men, Moses and Elijah, [31]appeared in glorious splendour, talking with Jesus. They spoke about his departure, which he was about to bring to fulfilment at Jerusalem. [32]Peter and his companions were very sleepy, but when they became fully awake, they saw his glory and the two men standing with him. [33]As the men were leaving Jesus, Peter said to him, "Master, it is good for us to be here. Let us put up three shelters—one for you, one for Moses and one for Elijah." (He did not know what he was saying.)

[34]While he was speaking, a cloud appeared and enveloped them, and they were afraid as they entered the cloud. [35]A voice came from the cloud, saying, "This is my Son, whom I have chosen; listen to him." [36]When the voice had spoken, they found that Jesus was alone. The disciples kept this to themselves, and told no-one at that time what they had seen.

The Healing of a Boy With an Evil Spirit

37The next day, when they came down from the mountain, a
large crowd met him. 38A man in the crowd called out, "Teacher, I
beg you to look at my son, for he is my only child. 39A spirit seizes
him and he suddenly screams; it throws him into convulsions so
that he foams at the mouth. It scarcely ever leaves him and is
destroying him. 40I begged your disciples to drive it out, but they
could not."
41"O unbelieving and perverse generation," Jesus replied, "how
long shall I stay with you and put up with you? Bring your son
here."
42Even while the boy was coming, the demon threw him to the
ground in a convulsion. But Jesus rebuked the evil spirit, healed
the boy and gave him back to his father. 43And they were all
amazed at the greatness of God.
While everyone was marvelling at all that Jesus did, he said to
his disciples, 44"Listen carefully to what I am about to tell you: The
Son of Man is going to be betrayed into the hands of men." 45But
they did not understand what this meant. It was hidden from
them, so that they did not grasp it, and they were afraid to ask him
about it.

Who Will Be the Greatest?

46An argument started among the disciples as to which of them
would be the greatest. 47Jesus, knowing their thoughts, took a little
child and made him stand beside him. 48Then he said to them,
"Whoever welcomes this little child in my name welcomes me; and
whoever welcomes me welcomes the one who sent me. For he
who is least among you all—he is the greatest."
49"Master," said John, "we saw a man driving out demons in
your name and we tried to stop him, because he is not one of us."
50"Do not stop him," Jesus said, "for whoever is not against you
is for you."

Samaritan Opposition

51As the time approached for him to be taken up to heaven, Jesus
resolutely set out for Jerusalem. 52And he sent messengers on
ahead, who went into a Samaritan village to get things ready for
him; 53but the people there did not welcome him, because he was
heading for Jerusalem. 54When the disciples James and John saw

this, they asked, "Lord, do you want us to call fire down from
heaven to destroy them?" 55 But Jesus turned and rebuked them,
56 and they went to another village.

The Cost of Following Jesus

57 As they were walking along the road, a man said to him, "I will
follow you wherever you go."
58 Jesus replied, "Foxes have holes and birds of the air have nests,
but the Son of Man has nowhere to lay his head."
59 He said to another man, "Follow me."
But the man replied, "Lord, first let me go and bury my father."
60 Jesus said to him, "Let the dead bury their own dead, but you
go and proclaim the kingdom of God."
61 Still another said, "I will follow you, Lord; but first let me go
back and say good-bye to my family."
62 Jesus replied, "No-one who puts his hand to the plough and
looks back is fit for service in the kingdom of God."

Jesus Sends Out the Seventy-two

10 After this the Lord appointed seventy-two others and sent
them two by two ahead of him to every town and place
where he was about to go. 2 He told them, "The harvest is plentiful,
but the workers are few. Ask the Lord of the harvest, therefore, to
send out workers into his harvest field. 3 Go! I am sending you out
like lambs among wolves. 4 Do not take a purse or bag or sandals;
and do not greet anyone on the road.
5 "When you enter a house, first say, 'Peace to this house.' 6 If a
man of peace is there, your peace will rest on him; if not, it will
return to you. 7 Stay in that house, eating and drinking whatever
they give you, for the worker deserves his wages. Do not move
around from house to house.
8 "When you enter a town and are welcomed, eat what is set
before you. 9 Heal the sick who are there and tell them, 'The
kingdom of God is near you.' 10 But when you enter a town and are
not welcomed, go into its streets and say, 11 'Even the dust of your
town that sticks to our feet we wipe off against you. Yet be sure of
this: The kingdom of God is near.' 12 I tell you, it will be more
bearable on that day for Sodom than for that town.
13 "Woe to you, Korazin! Woe to you, Bethsaida! For if the
miracles that were performed in you had been performed in Tyre

and Sidon, they would have repented long ago, sitting in sackcloth
and ashes. [14]But it will be more bearable for Tyre and Sidon at the
judgment than for you. [15]And you, Capernaum, will you be lifted
up to the skies? No, you will go down to the depths.
[16]"He who listens to you listens to me; he who rejects you rejects
me; but he who rejects me rejects him who sent me."
[17]The seventy-two returned with joy and said, "Lord, even the
demons submit to us in your name."
[18]He replied, "I saw Satan fall like lightning from heaven. [19]I
have given you authority to trample on snakes and scorpions and
to overcome all the power of the enemy; nothing will harm you.
[20]However, do not rejoice that the spirits submit to you, but rejoice
that your names are written in heaven."
[21]At that time Jesus, full of joy through the Holy Spirit, said, "I
praise you, Father, Lord of heaven and earth, because you have
hidden these things from the wise and learned, and revealed them
to little children. Yes, Father, for this was your good pleasure.
[22]"All things have been committed to me by my Father. No-one
knows who the Son is except the Father, and no-one knows who
the Father is except the Son and those to whom the Son chooses to
reveal him."
[23]Then he turned to his disciples and said privately, "Blessed are
the eyes that see what you see. [24]For I tell you that many prophets
and kings wanted to see what you see but did not see it, and to hear
what you hear but did not hear it."

The Parable of the Good Samaritan

[25]On one occasion an expert in the law stood up to test Jesus.
"Teacher," he asked, "what must I do to inherit eternal life?"
[26]"What is written in the Law?" he replied. "How do you read
it?"
[27]He answered: "'Love the Lord your God with all your heart
and with all your soul and with all your strength and with all your
mind'; and, 'Love your neighbour as yourself.'"
[28]"You have answered correctly," Jesus replied. "Do this and
you will live."
[29]But he wanted to justify himself, so he asked Jesus, "And who
is my neighbour?"
[30]In reply Jesus said: "A man was going down from Jerusalem to
Jericho, when he fell into the hands of robbers. They stripped him
of his clothes, beat him and went away, leaving him half-dead. [31]A

priest happened to be going down the same road, and when he
saw the man, he passed by on the other side. 32So too, a Levite,
when he came to the place and saw him, passed by on the other
side. 33But a Samaritan, as he travelled, came where the man was;
and when he saw him, he took pity on him. 34He went to him and
bandaged his wounds, pouring on oil and wine. Then he put the
man on his own donkey, brought him to an inn and took care of
him. 35The next day he took out two silver coins and gave them to
the innkeeper. 'Look after him,' he said, 'and when I return, I will
reimburse you for any extra expense you may have.'
36"Which of these three do you think was a neighbour to the man
who fell into the hands of robbers?"
37The expert in the law replied, "The one who had mercy on
him."

Jesus told him, "Go and do likewise."

He went to him and bandaged his wounds (10:34)

At the Home of Martha and Mary

38 As Jesus and his disciples were on their way, he came to a
village where a woman named Martha opened her home to him.
39 She had a sister called Mary, who sat at the Lord's feet listening to
what he said. 40 But Martha was distracted by all the preparations
that had to be made. She came to him and asked, "Lord, don't you
care that my sister has left me to do the work by myself? Tell her to
help me!"

41 "Martha, Martha," the Lord answered, "you are worried and
upset about many things, 42 but only one thing is needed. Mary has
chosen what is better, and it will not be taken away from her."

Jesus' Teaching on Prayer

11 One day Jesus was praying in a certain place. When he
finished, one of his disciples said to him, "Lord, teach us to
pray, just as John taught his disciples."

2 He said to them, "When you pray, say:

"'Father,
hallowed be your name,
your kingdom come.
3 Give us each day our daily bread.
4 Forgive us our sins,
    for we also forgive everyone who sins against us.
And lead us not into temptation.'"

5 Then he said to them, "Suppose one of you has a friend, and he
goes to him at midnight and says, 'Friend, lend me three loaves of
bread, 6 because a friend of mine on a journey has come to me, and I
have nothing to set before him.'

7 "Then the one inside answers, 'Don't bother me. The door is
already locked, and my children are with me in bed. I can't get up
and give you anything.' 8 I tell you, though he will not get up and
give him the bread because he is his friend, yet because of the
man's boldness he will get up and give him as much as he needs.

9 "So I say to you: Ask and it will be given to you; seek and you
will find; knock and the door will be opened to you. 10 For everyone
who asks receives; he who seeks finds; and to him who knocks, the
door will be opened.

11 "Which of you fathers, if your son asks for a fish, will give him a

snake instead? 12Or if he asks for an egg, will give him a scorpion?
13If you then, though you are evil, know how to give good gifts to
your children, how much more will your Father in heaven give the
Holy Spirit to those who ask him!"

Jesus and Beelzebub

14Jesus was driving out a demon that was mute. When the
demon left, the man who had been mute spoke, and the crowd
was amazed. 15But some of them said, "By Beelzebub, the prince of
demons, he is driving out demons." 16Others tested him by asking
for a sign from heaven.

17Jesus knew their thoughts and said to them: "Any kingdom
divided against itself will be ruined, and a house divided against
itself will fall. 18If Satan is divided against himself, how can his
kingdom stand? I say this because you claim that I drive out
demons by Beelzebub. 19Now if I drive out demons by Beelzebub,
by whom do your followers drive them out? So then, they will be
your judges. 20But if I drive out demons by the finger of God, then
the kingdom of God has come to you.

21"When a strong man, fully armed, guards his own house, his
possessions are safe. 22But when someone stronger attacks and
overpowers him, he takes away the armour in which the man
trusted and divides up the spoils.

23"He who is not with me is against me, and he who does not
gather with me, scatters.

24"When an evil spirit comes out of a man, it goes through arid
places seeking rest and does not find it. Then it says, 'I will return
to the house I left.' 25When it arrives, it finds the house swept clean
and put in order. 26Then it goes and takes seven other spirits more
wicked than itself, and they go in and live there. And the final
condition of that man is worse than the first."

27As Jesus was saying these things, a woman in the crowd called
out, "Blessed is the mother who gave you birth and nursed you."

28He replied, "Blessed rather are those who hear the word of
God and obey it."

The Sign of Jonah

29As the crowds increased, Jesus said, "This is a wicked genera-
tion. It asks for a miraculous sign, but none will be given it except

the sign of Jonah. 30For as Jonah was a sign to the Ninevites, so also
will the Son of Man be to this generation. 31The Queen of the South
will rise at the judgment with the men of this generation and
condemn them; for she came from the ends of the earth to listen to
Solomon's wisdom, and now one greater than Solomon is here.
32The men of Nineveh will stand up at the judgment with this
generation and condemn it; for they repented at the preaching of
Jonah, and now one greater than Jonah is here.

The Lamp of the Body

33"No-one lights a lamp and puts it in a place where it will be
hidden, or under a bowl. Instead he puts it on its stand, so that
those who come in may see the light. 34Your eye is the lamp of your
body. When your eyes are good, your whole body also is full of
light. But when they are bad, your body also is full of darkness.
35See to it, then, that the light within you is not darkness.
36Therefore, if your whole body is full of light, and no part of it
dark, it will be completely lighted, as when the light of a lamp
shines on you."

Six Woes

37When Jesus had finished speaking, a Pharisee invited him to
eat with him; so he went in and reclined at the table. 38But the
Pharisee, noticing that Jesus did not first wash before the meal,
was surprised.

39Then the Lord said to him, "Now then, you Pharisees clean the
outside of the cup and dish, but inside you are full of greed and
wickedness. 40You foolish people! Did not the one who made the
outside make the inside also? 41But give what is inside ⌞the dish⌟ to
the poor, and everything will be clean for you.

42"Woe to you Pharisees, because you give God a tenth of your
mint, rue and all other kinds of garden herbs, but you neglect
justice and the love of God. You should have practised the latter
without leaving the former undone.

43"Woe to you Pharisees, because you love the most important
seats in the synagogues and greetings in the market-places.

44"Woe to you, because you are like unmarked graves, which
men walk over without knowing it."

45One of the experts in the law answered him, "Teacher, when
you say these things, you insult us also."
46Jesus replied, "And you experts in the law, woe to you,
because you load people down with burdens they can hardly
carry, and you yourselves will not lift one finger to help them.
47"Woe to you, because you build tombs for the prophets, and it
was your forefathers who killed them. 48So you testify that you
approve of what your forefathers did; they killed the prophets,
and you build their tombs. 49Because of this, God in his wisdom
said, 'I will send them prophets and apostles, some of whom they
will kill and others they will persecute.' 50Therefore this generation
will be held responsible for the blood of all the prophets that has
been shed since the beginning of the world, 51from the blood of
Abel to the blood of Zechariah, who was killed between the altar
and the sanctuary. Yes, I tell you, this generation will be held
responsible for it all.
52"Woe to you experts in the law, because you have taken away
the key to knowledge. You yourselves have not entered, and you
have hindered those who were entering."
53When Jesus left there, the Pharisees and the teachers of the law
began to oppose him fiercely and to besiege him with questions,
54waiting to catch him in something he might say.

Warnings and Encouragements

12 Meanwhile, when a crowd of many thousands had
gathered, so that they were trampling on one another,
Jesus began to speak first to his disciples, saying: "Be on your
guard against the yeast of the Pharisees, which is hypocrisy.
2There is nothing concealed that will not be disclosed, or hidden
that will not be made known. 3What you have said in the dark will
be heard in the daylight, and what you have whispered in the ear
in the inner rooms will be proclaimed from the roofs.
4"I tell you, my friends, do not be afraid of those who kill the
body and after that can do no more. 5But I will show you whom
you should fear: Fear him who, after the killing of the body, has
power to throw you into hell. Yes, I tell you, fear him. 6Are not five
sparrows sold for two pennies? Yet not one of them is forgotten by
God. 7Indeed, the very hairs of your head are all numbered. Don't
be afraid; you are worth more than many sparrows.
8"I tell you, whoever acknowledges me before men, the Son of

Man will also acknowledge him before the angels of God. 9But he
who disowns me before men will be disowned before the angels of
God. 10And everyone who speaks a word against the Son of Man
will be forgiven, but anyone who blasphemes against the Holy
Spirit will not be forgiven.
11"When you are brought before synagogues, rulers and author-
ities, do not worry about how you will defend yourselves or what
you will say, 12for the Holy Spirit will teach you at that time what
you should say."

The Parable of the Rich Fool

13Someone in the crowd said to him, "Teacher, tell my brother to
divide the inheritance with me."
14Jesus replied, "Man, who appointed me a judge or an arbiter
between you?" 15Then he said to them, "Watch out! Be on your
guard against all kinds of greed; a man's life does not consist in the
abundance of his possessions."
16And he told them this parable: "The ground of a certain rich
man produced a good crop. 17He thought to himself, 'What shall I
do? I have no place to store my crops.'
18"Then he said, 'This is what I'll do. I will tear down my barns
and build bigger ones, and there I will store all my grain and my
goods. 19And I'll say to myself, "You have plenty of good things
laid up for many years. Take life easy; eat, drink and be merry."'
20"But God said to him, 'You fool! This very night your life will
be demanded from you. Then who will get what you have pre-
pared for yourself?'
21"This is how it will be with anyone who stores up things for
himself but is not rich towards God."

Do Not Worry

22Then Jesus said to his disciples: "Therefore I tell you, do not
worry about your life, what you will eat; or about your body, what
you will wear. 23Life is more than food, and the body more than
clothes. 24Consider the ravens: They do not sow or reap, they have
no storeroom or barn; yet God feeds them. And how much more
valuable you are than birds! 25Who of you by worrying can add a
single hour to his life? 26Since you cannot do this very little thing,
why do you worry about the rest?

27"Consider how the lilies grow. They do not labour or spin. Yet
I tell you, not even Solomon in all his splendour was dressed like
one of these. 28If that is how God clothes the grass of the field,
which is here today, and tomorrow is thrown into the fire, how
much more will he clothe you, O you of little faith! 29And do not set
your heart on what you will eat or drink; do not worry about it.
30For the pagan world runs after all such things, and your Father
knows that you need them. 31But seek his kingdom, and these
things will be given to you as well.
32"Do not be afraid, little flock, for your Father has been pleased
to give you the kingdom. 33Sell your possessions and give to the
poor. Provide purses for yourselves that will not wear out, a
treasure in heaven that will not be exhausted, where no thief
comes near and no moth destroys. 34For where your treasure is,
there your heart will be also.

Watchfulness

35"Be dressed ready for service and keep your lamps burning,
36like men waiting for their master to return from a wedding
banquet, so that when he comes and knocks they can immediately
open the door for him. 37It will be good for those servants whose
master finds them watching when he comes. I tell you the truth, he
will dress himself to serve, will have them recline at the table and
will come and wait on them. 38It will be good for those servants
whose master finds them ready, even if he comes in the second or
third watch of the night. 39But understand this: If the owner of the
house had known at what hour the thief was coming, he would not
have let his house be broken into. 40You also must be ready,
because the Son of Man will come at an hour when you do not
expect him."
41Peter asked, "Lord, are you telling this parable to us, or to
everyone?"
42The Lord answered, "Who then is the faithful and wise mana-
ger, whom the master puts in charge of his servants to give them
their food allowance at the proper time? 43It will be good for that
servant whom the master finds doing so when he returns. 44I tell
you the truth, he will put him in charge of all his possessions. 45But
suppose the servant says to himself, 'My master is taking a long
time in coming,' and he then begins to beat the menservants and
maidservants and to eat and drink and get drunk. 46The master of

that servant will come on a day when he does not expect him and at
an hour he is not aware of. He will cut him to pieces and assign him
a place with the unbelievers.
[47]"That servant who knows his master's will and does not get
ready or does not do what his master wants will be beaten with
many blows. [48]But the one who does not know and does things
deserving punishment will be beaten with few blows. From every-
one who has been given much, much will be demanded; and from
the one who has been entrusted with much, much more will be
asked.

Not Peace but Division

[49]"I have come to bring fire on the earth, and how I wish it were
already kindled! [50]But I have a baptism to undergo, and how
distressed I am until it is completed! [51]Do you think I came to bring
peace on earth? No, I tell you, but division. [52]From now on there
will be five in one family divided against each other, three against
two and two against three. [53]They will be divided, father against
son and son against father, mother against daughter and daughter
against mother, mother-in-law against daughter-in-law and
daughter-in-law against mother-in-law."

Interpreting the Times

[54]He said to the crowd: "When you see a cloud rising in the west,
immediately you say, 'It's going to rain,' and it does. [55]And when
the south wind blows, you say, 'It's going to be hot,' and it is.
[56]Hypocrites! You know how to interpret the appearance of the
earth and the sky. How is it that you don't know how to interpret
this present time?
[57]"Why don't you judge for yourselves what is right? [58]As you
are going with your adversary to the magistrate, try hard to be
reconciled to him on the way, or he may drag you off to the judge,
and the judge turn you over to the officer, and the officer throw
you into prison. [59]I tell you, you will not get out until you have paid
the last penny."

Repent or Perish

13 Now there were some present at that time who told Jesus
about the Galileans whose blood Pilate had mixed with
their sacrifices. 2Jesus answered, "Do you think that these Gali-
leans were worse sinners than all the other Galileans because they
suffered this way? 3I tell you, no! But unless you repent, you too
will all perish. 4Or those eighteen who died when the tower in
Siloam fell on them—do you think they were more guilty than all
the others living in Jerusalem? 5I tell you, no! But unless you
repent, you too will all perish."
6Then he told this parable: "A man had a fig-tree, planted in his
vineyard, and he went to look for fruit on it, but did not find any.
7So he said to the man who took care of the vineyard, 'For three
years now I've been coming to look for fruit on this fig-tree and
haven't found any. Cut it down! Why should it use up the soil?'
8" 'Sir,' the man replied, 'leave it alone for one more year, and I'll
dig round it and fertilise it. 9If it bears fruit next year, fine! If not,
then cut it down.' "

A Crippled Woman Healed on the Sabbath

10On a Sabbath Jesus was teaching in one of the synagogues,
11and a woman was there who had been crippled by a spirit for
eighteen years. She was bent over and could not straighten up at
all. 12When Jesus saw her, he called her forward and said to her,
"Woman, you are set free from your infirmity." 13Then he put his
hands on her, and immediately she straightened up and praised
God.
14Indignant because Jesus had healed on the Sabbath, the syna-
gogue ruler said to the people, "There are six days for work. So
come and be healed on those days, not on the Sabbath."
15The Lord answered him, "You hypocrites! Doesn't each of you
on the Sabbath untie his ox or donkey from the stall and lead it out
to give it water? 16Then should not this woman, a daughter of
Abraham, whom Satan has kept bound for eighteen long years, be
set free on the Sabbath day from what bound her?"
17When he said this, all his opponents were humiliated, but the
people were delighted with all the wonderful things he was doing.

The Parables of the Mustard Seed and the Yeast

[18]Then Jesus asked, "What is the kingdom of God like? What
shall I compare it to? [19]It is like a mustard seed, which a man took
and planted in his garden. It grew and became a tree, and the birds
of the air perched in its branches."

The birds of the air perched in its branches (13:19)

[20]Again he asked, "What shall I compare the kingdom of God to?
[21]It is like yeast that a woman took and mixed into a large amount of
flour until it worked all through the dough."

The Narrow Door

[22]Then Jesus went through the towns and villages, teaching as

he made his way to Jerusalem. [23]Someone asked him, "Lord, are
only a few people going to be saved?"
He said to them, [24]"Make every effort to enter through the
narrow door, because many, I tell you, will try to enter and will not
be able to. [25]Once the owner of the house gets up and closes the
door, you will stand outside knocking and pleading, 'Sir, open the
door for us.'
"But he will answer, 'I don't know you or where you come
from.'
[26]"Then you will say, 'We ate and drank with you, and you
taught in our streets.'
[27]"But he will reply, 'I don't know you or where you come from.
Away from me, all you evildoers!'
[28]"There will be weeping there, and gnashing of teeth, when
you see Abraham, Isaac and Jacob and all the prophets in the
kingdom of God, but you yourselves thrown out. [29]People will
come from east and west and north and south, and will take their
places at the feast in the kingdom of God. [30]Indeed there are those
who are last who will be first, and first who will be last."

Jesus' Sorrow for Jerusalem

[31]At that time some Pharisees came to Jesus and said to him,
"Leave this place and go somewhere else. Herod wants to kill
you."
[32]He replied, "Go tell that fox, 'I will drive out demons and heal
people today and tomorrow, and on the third day I will reach my
goal.' [33]In any case, I must keep going today and tomorrow and the
next day—for surely no prophet can die outside Jerusalem!
[34]"O Jerusalem, Jerusalem, you who kill the prophets and stone
those sent to you, how often I have longed to gather your children
together, as a hen gathers her chicks under her wings, but you
were not willing! [35]Look, your house is left to you desolate. I tell
you, you will not see me again until you say, 'Blessed is he who
comes in the name of the Lord.'"

Jesus at a Pharisee's House

14 One Sabbath, when Jesus went to eat in the house of a
prominent Pharisee, he was being carefully watched.
[2]There in front of him was a man suffering from dropsy. [3]Jesus
asked the Pharisees and experts in the law, "Is it lawful to heal on

the Sabbath or not?" 4But they remained silent. So taking hold of
the man, he healed him and sent him away.
5Then he asked them, "If one of you has a son or an ox that falls
into a well on the Sabbath day, will you not immediately pull him
out?" 6And they had nothing to say.
7When he noticed how the guests picked the places of honour at
the table, he told them this parable: 8"When someone invites you
to a wedding feast, do not take the place of honour, for a person
more distinguished than you may have been invited. 9If so, the
host who invited both of you will come and say to you, 'Give this
man your seat.' Then, humiliated, you will have to take the least
important place. 10But when you are invited, take the lowest place,
so that when your host comes, he will say to you, 'Friend, move up
to a better place.' Then you will be honoured in the presence of all
your fellow guests. 11For everyone who exalts himself will be
humbled, and he who humbles himself will be exalted."
12Then Jesus said to his host, "When you give a luncheon or
dinner, do not invite your friends, your brothers or relatives, or
your rich neighbours; if you do, they may invite you back and so
you will be repaid. 13But when you give a banquet, invite the poor,
the crippled, the lame, the blind, 14and you will be blessed.
Although they cannot repay you, you will be repaid at the resur-
rection of the righteous."

The Parable of the Great Banquet

15When one of those at the table with him heard this, he said to
Jesus, "Blessed is the man who will eat at the feast in the kingdom
of God."
16Jesus replied: "A certain man was preparing a great banquet
and invited many guests. 17At the time of the banquet he sent his
servant to tell those who had been invited, 'Come, for everything
is now ready.'
18"But they all alike began to make excuses. The first said, 'I have
just bought a field, and I must go and see it. Please excuse me.'
19"Another said, 'I have just bought five yoke of oxen, and I'm
on my way to try them out. Please excuse me.'
20"Still another said, 'I have just got married, so I can't come.'
21"The servant came back and reported this to his master. Then
the owner of the house became angry and ordered his servant, 'Go
out quickly into the streets and alleys of the town and bring in the
poor, the crippled, the blind and the lame.'

22"'Sir,' the servant said, 'what you ordered has been done, but
there is still room.'
23"Then the master told his servant, 'Go out to the roads and
country lanes and make them come in, so that my house will be
full. 24I tell you, not one of those men who were invited will get a
taste of my banquet.'"

The Cost of Being a Disciple

25Large crowds were travelling with Jesus, and turning to them
he said: 26"If anyone comes to me and does not hate his father and
mother, his wife and children, his brothers and sisters—yes, even
his own life—he cannot be my disciple. 27And anyone who does
not carry his cross and follow me cannot be my disciple.
28"Suppose one of you wants to build a tower. Will he not first sit
down and estimate the cost to see if he has enough money to
complete it? 29For if he lays the foundation and is not able to finish
it, everyone who sees it will ridicule him, 30saying, 'This fellow
began to build and was not able to finish.'
31"Or suppose a king is about to go to war against another king.
Will he not first sit down and consider whether he is able with ten
thousand men to oppose the one coming against him with twenty
thousand? 32If he is not able, he will send a delegation while the
other is still a long way off and will ask for terms of peace. 33In the
same way, any of you who does not give up everything he has
cannot be my disciple.
34"Salt is good, but if it loses its saltiness, how can it be made
salty again? 35It is fit neither for the soil nor for the manure heap; it
is thrown out.
"He who has ears to hear, let him hear."

The Parable of the Lost Sheep

15 Now the tax collectors and "sinners" were all gathering
round to hear him. 2But the Pharisees and the teachers of
the law muttered, "This man welcomes sinners, and eats with
them."
3Then Jesus told them this parable: 4"Suppose one of you has a
hundred sheep and loses one of them. Does he not leave the
ninety-nine in the open country and go after the lost sheep until he

He joyfully puts it on his shoulders (15:5)

finds it? 5And when he finds it, he joyfully puts it on his shoulders
6and goes home. Then he calls his friends and neighbours together
and says, 'Rejoice with me; I have found my lost sheep.' 7I tell you
that in the same way there will be more rejoicing in heaven over
one sinner who repents than over ninety-nine righteous persons
who do not need to repent.

The Parable of the Lost Coin

8"Or suppose a woman has ten silver coins and loses one. Does
she not light a lamp, sweep the house and search carefully until
she finds it? 9And when she finds it, she calls her friends and
neighbours together and says, 'Rejoice with me; I have found my
lost coin.' 10In the same way, I tell you, there is rejoicing in the

I have found my lost coin (15:9)

presence of the angels of God over one sinner who repents."

The Parable of the Lost Son

[11]Jesus continued: "There was a man who had two sons. [12]The
younger one said to his father, 'Father, give me my share of the
estate.' So he divided his property between them.

[13]"Not long after that, the younger son got together all he had,
set off for a distant country and there squandered his wealth in
wild living. [14]After he had spent everything, there was a severe
famine in that whole country, and he began to be in need. [15]So he
went and hired himself out to a citizen of that country, who sent
him to his fields to feed pigs. [16]He longed to fill his stomach with
the pods that the pigs were eating, but no-one gave him anything.

[17]"When he came to his senses, he said, 'How many of my
father's hired men have food to spare, and here I am starving to
death! [18]I will set out and go back to my father and say to him:
Father, I have sinned against heaven and against you. [19]I am no
longer worthy to be called your son; make me like one of your
hired men.' [20]So he got up and went to his father.

"But while he was still a long way off, his father saw him and
was filled with compassion for him; he ran to his son, threw his
arms around him and kissed him.

[21]"The son said to him, 'Father, I have sinned against heaven
and against you. I am no longer worthy to be called your son.'

[22]"But the father said to his servants, 'Quick! Bring the best robe
and put it on him. Put a ring on his finger and sandals on his feet.
[23]Bring the fattened calf and kill it. Let's have a feast and celebrate.
[24]For this son of mine was dead and is alive again; he was lost and is
found.' So they began to celebrate.

[25]"Meanwhile, the older son was in the field. When he came
near the house, he heard music and dancing. [26]So he called one of
the servants and asked him what was going on. [27]'Your brother has
come,' he replied, 'and your father has killed the fattened calf
because he has him back safe and sound.'

[28]"The older brother became angry and refused to go in. So his
father went out and pleaded with him. [29]But he answered his
father, 'Look! All these years I've been slaving for you and never
disobeyed your orders. Yet you never gave me even a young goat
so I could celebrate with my friends. [30]But when this son of yours
who has squandered your property with prostitutes comes home,
you kill the fattened calf for him!'

31"'My son,' the father said, 'you are always with me, and
everything I have is yours. 32But we had to celebrate and be glad,
because this brother of yours was dead and is alive again; he was
lost and is found.'"

The Parable of the Shrewd Manager

16 Jesus told his disciples: "There was a rich man whose
manager was accused of wasting his possessions. 2So he
called him in and asked him, 'What is this I hear about you? Give
an account of your management, because you cannot be manager
any longer.'
3"The manager said to himself, 'What shall I do now? My master
is taking away my job. I'm not strong enough to dig, and I'm
ashamed to beg—4I know what I'll do so that, when I lose my job
here, people will welcome me into their houses.'
5"So he called in each one of his master's debtors. He asked the
first, 'How much do you owe my master?'
6"'Eight hundred gallons of olive oil,' he replied.
"The manager told him, 'Take your bill, sit down quickly, and
make it four hundred.'
7"Then he asked the second, 'And how much do you owe?'
"'A thousand bushels of wheat,' he replied.
"He told him, 'Take your bill and make it eight hundred.'
8"The master commended the dishonest manager because he
had acted shrewdly. For the people of this world are more shrewd
in dealing with their own kind than are the people of the light. 9I
tell you, use worldly wealth to gain friends for yourselves, so that
when it is gone, you will be welcomed into eternal dwellings.
10"Whoever can be trusted with very little can also be trusted
with much, and whoever is dishonest with very little will also be
dishonest with much. 11So if you have not been trustworthy in
handling worldly wealth, who will trust you with true riches?
12And if you have not been trustworthy with someone else's
property, who will give you property of your own?
13"No servant can serve two masters. Either he will hate the one
and love the other, or he will be devoted to the one and despise the
other. You cannot serve both God and Money."
14The Pharisees, who loved money, heard all this and were
sneering at Jesus. 15He said to them, "You are the ones who justify
yourselves in the eyes of men, but God knows your hearts. What is
highly valued among men is detestable in God's sight.

Additional Teachings

16"The Law and the Prophets were proclaimed until John. Since
that time, the good news of the kingdom of God is being preached,
and everyone is forcing his way into it. 17It is easier for heaven and
earth to disappear than for the least stroke of a pen to drop out of
the Law.
18"Anyone who divorces his wife and marries another woman
commits adultery, and the man who marries a divorced woman
commits adultery.

The Rich Man and Lazarus

19"There was a rich man who was dressed in purple and fine
linen and lived in luxury every day. 20At his gate was laid a beggar
named Lazarus, covered with sores 21and longing to eat what fell
from the rich man's table. Even the dogs came and licked his sores.

A beggar named Lazarus (16:20)

22"The time came when the beggar died and the angels carried
him to Abraham's side. The rich man also died and was buried.
23In hell, where he was in torment, he looked up and saw Abraham
far away, with Lazarus by his side. 24So he called to him, 'Father

Abraham, have pity on me and send Lazarus to dip the tip of his
finger in water and cool my tongue, because I am in agony in this
fire.'
25"But Abraham replied, 'Son, remember that in your lifetime
you received your good things, while Lazarus received bad things,
but now he is comforted here and you are in agony. 26And besides
all this, between us and you a great chasm has been fixed, so that
those who want to go from here to you cannot, nor can anyone
cross over from there to us.'
27"He answered, 'Then I beg you, father, send Lazarus to my
father's house, 28for I have five brothers. Let him warn them, so
that they will not also come to this place of torment.'
29"Abraham replied, 'They have Moses and the Prophets; let
them listen to them.'
30" 'No father Abraham,' he said, 'but if someone from the dead
goes to them, they will repent.'
31"He said to him, 'If they do not listen to Moses and the
Prophets, they will not be convinced even if someone rises from
the dead.' "

Sin, Faith, Duty

17 Jesus said to his disciples: "Things that cause people to sin
are bound to come, but woe to that person through whom
they come. 2It would be better for him to be thrown into the sea
with a millstone tied round his neck than for him to cause one of
these little ones to sin. 3So watch yourselves.
"If your brother sins, rebuke him, and if he repents, forgive him.
4If he sins against you seven times in a day, and seven times comes
back to you and says, 'I repent,' forgive him."
5The apostles said to the Lord, "Increase our faith!"
6He replied, "If you have faith as small as a mustard seed, you
can say to this mulberry tree, 'Be uprooted and planted in the sea,'
and it will obey you.
7"Suppose one of you had a servant ploughing or looking after
the sheep. Would he say to the servant when he comes in from the
field, 'Come along now and sit down to eat'? 8Would he not rather
say, 'Prepare my supper, get yourself ready and wait on me while I
eat and drink; after that you may eat and drink'? 9Would he thank
the servant because he did what he was told to do? 10So you also,
when you have done everything you were told to do, should say,
'We are unworthy servants; we have only done our duty.' "

Ten Healed of Leprosy

[11]Now on his way to Jerusalem, Jesus travelled along the border
between Samaria and Galilee. [12]As he was going into a village, ten
men who had leprosy met him. They stood at a distance [13]and
called out in a loud voice, "Jesus, Master, have pity on us!"
[14]When he saw them, he said, "Go, show yourselves to the
priests." And as they went, they were cleansed.
[15]One of them, when he saw he was healed, came back, praising
God in a loud voice. [16]He threw himself at Jesus' feet and thanked
him—and he was a Samaritan.
[17]Jesus asked, "Were not all ten cleansed? Where are the other
nine? [18]Was no-one found to return and give praise to God except
this foreigner?" [19]Then he said to him, "Rise and go; your faith has
made you well."

The Coming of the Kingdom of God

[20]Once, having been asked by the Pharisees when the kingdom
of God would come, Jesus replied, "The kingdom of God does not
come with your careful observation, [21]nor will people say, 'Here it
is,' or 'There it is,' because the kingdom of God is within you."
[22]Then he said to his disciples, "The time is coming when you
will long to see one of the days of the Son of Man, but you will not
see it. [23]Men will tell you, 'There he is!' or 'Here he is!' Do not go
running off after them. [24]For the Son of Man in his day will be like
the lightning, which flashes and lights up the sky from one end to
the other. [25]But first he must suffer many things and be rejected by
this generation.
[26]"Just as it was in the days of Noah, so also will it be in the days
of the Son of Man. [27]People were eating, drinking, marrying and
being given in marriage up to the day Noah entered the ark. Then
the flood came and destroyed them all.
[28]"It was the same in the days of Lot. People were eating and
drinking, buying and selling, planting and building. [29]But the day
Lot left Sodom, fire and sulphur rained down from heaven and
destroyed them all.
[30]"It will be just like this on the day the Son of Man is revealed.
[31]On that day no-one who is on the roof of his house, with his
goods inside, should go down to get them. Likewise, no-one in the
field should go back for anything. [32]Remember Lot's wife!
[33]Whoever tries to keep his life will lose it, and whoever loses his
life will preserve it. [34]I tell you, on that night two people will be in

one bed; one will be taken and the other left. 35Two women will be
grinding grain together; one will be taken and the other left."
37"Where, Lord?" they asked.
He replied, "Where there is a dead body, there the vultures will
gather."

The Parable of the Persistent Widow

18 Then Jesus told his disciples a parable to show them that
they should always pray and not give up. 2He said: "In a
certain town there was a judge who neither feared God nor cared
about men. 3And there was a widow in that town who kept coming
to him with the plea, 'Grant me justice against my adversary.'
4"For some time he refused. But finally he said to himself, 'Even
though I don't fear God or care about men, 5yet because this
widow keeps bothering me, I will see that she gets justice, so that
she won't eventually wear me out with her coming!'"
6And the Lord said, "Listen to what the unjust judge says. 7And
will not God bring about justice for his chosen ones, who cry out to
him day and night? Will he keep putting them off? 8I tell you, he
will see that they get justice, and quickly. However, when the Son
of Man comes, will he find faith on the earth?"

The Parable of the Pharisee and the Tax Collector

9To some who were confident of their own righteousness and
looked down on everybody else, Jesus told this parable: 10"Two
men went up to the temple to pray, one a Pharisee and the other a
tax collector. 11The Pharisee stood up and prayed about himself:
'God, I thank you that I am not like other men—robbers, evildoers,
adulterers—or even like this tax collector. 12I fast twice a week and
give a tenth of all I get.'
13"But the tax collector stood at a distance. He would not even
look up to heaven, but beat his breast and said, 'God, have mercy
on me, a sinner.'
14"I tell you that this man, rather than the other, went home
justified before God. For everyone who exalts himself will be
humbled, and he who humbles himself will be exalted."

The Little Children and Jesus

15People were also bringing babies to Jesus to have him touch
them. When the disciples saw this, they rebuked them. 16But Jesus

called the children to him and said, "Let the little children come to
me, and do not hinder them, for the kingdom of God belongs to
such as these. 17I tell you the truth, anyone who will not receive the
kingdom of God like a little child will never enter it."

The Rich Ruler

18A certain ruler asked him, "Good teacher, what must I do to
inherit eternal life?"
19"Why do you call me good?" Jesus answered. "No-one is
good—except God alone. 20You know the commandments: 'Do
not commit adultery, do not murder, do not steal, do not give false
testimony, honour your father and mother.' "
21"All these I have kept since I was a boy," he said.
22When Jesus heard this, he said to him, "You still lack one
thing. Sell everything you have and give to the poor, and you will
have treasure in heaven. Then come, follow me."
23When he heard this, he became very sad, because he was a
man of great wealth. 24Jesus looked at him and said, "How hard it
is for the rich to enter the kingdom of God! 25Indeed, it is easier for
a camel to go through the eye of a needle than for a rich man to
enter the kingdom of God."
26Those who heard this asked, "Who then can be saved?"
27Jesus replied, "What is impossible with men is possible with
God."
28Peter said to him, "We have left all we had to follow you!"
29"I tell you the truth," Jesus said to them, "no-one who has left
home or wife or brothers or parents or children for the sake of the
kingdom of God 30will fail to receive many times as much in this
age and, in the age to come, eternal life."

Jesus Again Predicts His Death

31Jesus took the Twelve aside and told them, "We are going up to
Jerusalem, and everything that is written by the prophets about
the Son of Man will be fulfilled. 32He will be turned over to the
Gentiles. They will mock him, insult him, spit on him, flog him
and kill him. 33On the third day he will rise again."
34The disciples did not understand any of this. Its meaning was
hidden from them, and they did not know what he was talking
about.

A Blind Beggar Receives His Sight

35As Jesus approached Jericho, a blind man was sitting by the
roadside begging. 36When he heard the crowd going by, he asked
what was happening. 37They told him, "Jesus of Nazareth is
passing by."
38He called out, "Jesus, Son of David, have mercy on me!"
39Those who led the way rebuked him and told him to be quiet,
but he shouted all the more, "Son of David, have mercy on me!"
40Jesus stopped and ordered the man to be brought to him.
When he came near, Jesus asked him, 41"What do you want me to
do for you?"

"Lord, I want to see," he replied.
42Jesus said to him, "Receive your sight; your faith has healed
you." 43Immediately he received his sight and followed Jesus,
praising God. When all the people saw it, they also praised God.

Zacchaeus the Tax Collector

19 Jesus entered Jericho and was passing through. 2A man
was there by the name of Zacchaeus; he was a chief tax
collector and was wealthy. 3He wanted to see who Jesus was, but
being a short man he could not, because of the crowd. 4So he ran
ahead and climbed a sycamore-fig tree to see him, since Jesus was
coming that way.

He climbed a sycamore-fig tree to see him (19:4)

5When Jesus reached the spot, he looked up and said to him,
"Zacchaeus, come down immediately. I must stay at your house
today." 6So he came down at once and welcomed him gladly.
7All the people saw this and began to mutter, "He has gone to be
the guest of a 'sinner'."
8But Zacchaeus stood up and said to the Lord, "Look, Lord!
Here and now I give half of my possessions to the poor, and if I
have cheated anybody out of anything, I will pay back four times
the amount."
9Jesus said to him, "Today salvation has come to this house,
because this man, too, is a son of Abraham. 10For the Son of Man
came to seek and to save what was lost."

The Parable of the Ten Minas

11While they were listening to this, he went on to tell them a
parable, because he was near Jerusalem and the people thought
that the kingdom of God was going to appear at once. 12He said: "A
man of noble birth went to a distant country to have himself
appointed king and then to return. 13So he called ten of his
servants and gave them ten minas. 'Put this money to work,' he
said, 'until I come back.'
14"But his subjects hated him and sent a delegation after him to
say, 'We don't want this man to be our king.'
15"He was made king, however, and returned home. Then he
sent for the servants to whom he had given the money, in order to
find out what they had gained with it.
16"The first one came and said, 'Sir, your mina has earned ten
more.'
17"'Well done, my good servant!' his master replied. 'Because
you have been trustworthy in a very small matter, take charge of
ten cities.'
18"The second came and said, 'Sir, your mina has earned five
more.'
19"His master answered, 'You take charge of five cities.'
20"Then another servant came and said, 'Sir, here is your mina; I
have kept it laid away in a piece of cloth. 21I was afraid of you,
because you are a hard man. You take out what you did not put in
and reap what you did not sow.'
22"His master replied, 'I will judge you by your own words, you
wicked servant! You knew, did you, that I am a hard man, taking
out what I did not put in, and reaping what I did not sow? 23Why

then didn't you put my money on deposit, so that when I came
back, I could have collected it with interest?'
24"Then he said to those standing by, 'Take his mina away from
him and give it to the one who has ten minas.'
25"'Sir,' they said, 'he already has ten!'
26"He replied, 'I tell you that to everyone who has, more will be
given, but as for the one who has nothing, even what he has will be
taken away. 27But those enemies of mine who did not want me to
be a king over them—bring them here and kill them in front of
me.'"

The Triumphal Entry

28After Jesus had said this, he went on ahead, going up to
Jerusalem. 29As he approached Bethphage and Bethany at the hill
called the Mount of Olives, he sent two of his disciples, saying to
them, 30"Go to the village ahead of you, and as you enter it, you
will find a colt tied there, which no-one has ever ridden. Untie it
and bring it here. 31If anyone asks you, 'Why are you untying it?'
tell him, 'The Lord needs it.'"
32Those who were sent ahead went and found it just as he had
told them. 33As they were untying the colt, its owners asked them,
"Why are you untying the colt?"
34They replied, "The Lord needs it."
35They brought it to Jesus, threw their cloaks on the colt and put
Jesus on it. 36As he went along, people spread their cloaks on the
road.
37When he came near the place where the road goes down the
Mount of Olives, the whole crowd of disciples began joyfully to
praise God in loud voices for all the miracles they had seen:

38"Blessed is the king who comes in the name of the Lord!"

"Peace in heaven and glory in the highest!"

39Some of the Pharisees in the crowd said to Jesus, "Teacher,
rebuke your disciples!"
40"I tell you," he replied, "if they keep quiet, the stones will cry
out."
41As he approached Jerusalem and saw the city, he wept over it
42and said, "If you, even you, had only known on this day what
would bring you peace—but now it is hidden from your eyes.

[43]The days will come upon you when your enemies will build an embankment against you and encircle you and hem you in on every side. [44]They will dash you to the ground, you and the children within your walls. They will not leave one stone on another, because you did not recognise the time of God's coming to you."

Jesus at the Temple

[45]Then he entered the temple area and began driving out those who were selling. [46]"It is written," he said to them, "'My house will be a house of prayer'; but you have made it 'a den of robbers'."

[47]Every day he was teaching at the temple. But the chief priests, the teachers of the law and the leaders among the people were trying to kill him. [48]Yet they could not find any way to do it, because all the people hung on his words.

The Authority of Jesus Questioned

20 One day as he was teaching the people in the temple courts and preaching the gospel, the chief priests and the teachers of the law, together with the elders, came up to him. [2]"Tell us by what authority you are doing these things," they said. "Who gave you this authority?"

[3]He replied, "I will also ask you a question. Tell me, [4]John's baptism—was it from heaven, or from men?"

[5]They discussed it among themselves and said, "If we say, 'From heaven', he will ask, 'Why didn't you believe him?' [6]But if we say, 'From men', all the people will stone us, because they are persuaded that John was a prophet."

[7]So they answered, "We don't know where it was from."

[8]Jesus said, "Neither will I tell you by what authority I am doing these things."

The Parable of the Tenants

[9]He went on to tell the people this parable: "A man planted a vineyard, rented it to some farmers and went away for a long time. [10]At harvest time he sent a servant to the tenants so they would give him some of the fruit of the vineyard. But the tenants beat him and sent him away empty-handed. [11]He sent another servant, but that one also they beat and treated shamefully and sent away

empty-handed. [12]He sent still a third, and they wounded him and threw him out.

[13]"Then the owner of the vineyard said, 'What shall I do? I will send my son, whom I love; perhaps they will respect him.'

[14]"But when the tenants saw him, they talked the matter over. 'This is the heir,' they said. 'Let's kill him, and the inheritance will be ours.' [15]So they threw him out of the vineyard and killed him.

"What then will the owner of the vineyard do to them? [16]He will come and kill those tenants and give the vineyard to others."

When the people heard this, they said, "May this never be!"

[17]Jesus looked directly at them and asked, "Then what is the meaning of that which is written:

"'The stone the builders rejected
has become the capstone'?

[18]Everyone who falls on that stone will be broken to pieces, but he on whom it falls will be crushed."

[19]The teachers of the law and the chief priests looked for a way to arrest him immediately, because they knew he had spoken this parable against them. But they were afraid of the people.

Paying Taxes to Caesar

[20]Keeping a close watch on him, they sent spies, who pretended to be honest. They hoped to catch Jesus in something he said so that they might hand him over to the power and authority of the governor. [21]So the spies questioned him: "Teacher, we know that you speak and teach what is right, and that you do not show partiality but teach the way of God in accordance with the truth. [22]Is it right for us to pay taxes to Caesar or not?"

[23]He saw through their duplicity and said to them, [24]"Show me a denarius. Whose portrait and inscription are on it?"

[25]"Caesar's," they replied.

He said to them, "Then give to Caesar what is Caesar's, and to God what is God's."

[26]They were unable to trap him in what he had said there in public. And astonished by his answer, they became silent.

The Resurrection and Marriage

[27]Some of the Sadducees, who say there is no resurrection, came

to Jesus with a question. 28"Teacher," they said, "Moses wrote for
us that if a man's brother dies and leaves a wife but no children, the
man must marry the widow and have children for his brother.
29Now there were seven brothers. The first one married a woman
and died childless. 30The second 31and then the third married her,
and in the same way the seven died, leaving no children. 32Finally,
the woman died too. 33Now then, at the resurrection whose wife
will she be, since the seven were married to her?"
34Jesus replied, "The people of this age marry and are given in
marriage. 35But those who are considered worthy of taking part in
that age and in the resurrection from the dead will neither marry
nor be given in marriage, 36and they can no longer die; for they are
like the angels. They are God's children, since they are children of
the resurrection. 37But in the account of the bush, even Moses
showed that the dead rise, for he calls the Lord 'the God of
Abraham, and the God of Isaac, and the God of Jacob'. 38He is not
the God of the dead, but of the living, for to him all are alive."
39Some of the teachers of the law responded, "Well said,
teacher!" 40And no-one dared to ask him any more questions.

Whose Son Is the Christ?

41Then Jesus said to them, "How is it that they say the Christ is
the Son of David? 42David himself declares in the Book of Psalms:

" 'The Lord said to my Lord:
"Sit at my right hand
43until I make your enemies
a footstool for your feet." '

44David calls him 'Lord'. How then can he be his son?"
45While all the people were listening, Jesus said to his disciples,
46"Beware of the teachers of the law. They like to walk around in
flowing robes and love to be greeted in the market-places and have
the most important seats in the synagogues and the places of
honour at banquets. 47They devour widows' houses and for a
show make lengthy prayers. Such men will be punished most
severely."

The Widow's Offering

21 As he looked up, Jesus saw the rich putting their gifts into
the temple treasury. 2He also saw a poor widow put in two

A poor widow put in two very small copper coins (21:2)

very small copper coins. [3]"I tell you the truth," he said, "this poor widow has put in more than all the others. [4]All these people gave their gifts out of their wealth; but she out of her poverty put in all she had to live on."

Signs of the End of the Age

[5]Some of his disciples were remarking about how the temple was adorned with beautiful stones and with gifts dedicated to God. But Jesus said, [6]"As for what you see here, the time will come when not one stone will be left on another; every one of them will be thrown down."

[7]"Teacher," they asked, "when will these things happen? And what will be the sign that they are about to take place?"

[8]He replied: "Watch out that you are not deceived. For many will come in my name, claiming, 'I am he,' and 'The time is near.' Do not follow them. [9]When you hear of wars and revolutions, do not be frightened. These things must happen first, but the end will not come right away."

[10]Then he said to them: "Nation will rise against nation, and kingdom against kingdom. [11]There will be great earthquakes, famines and pestilences in various places, and fearful events and great signs from heaven.

12"But before all this, they will lay hands on you and persecute
you. They will deliver you to synagogues and prisons, and you
will be brought before kings and governors, and all on account of
my name. 13This will result in your being witnesses to them. 14But
make up your mind not to worry beforehand how you will defend
yourselves. 15For I will give you words and wisdom that none of
your adversaries will be able to resist or contradict. 16You will be
betrayed even by parents, brothers, relatives and friends, and they
will put some of you to death. 17All men will hate you because of
me. 18But not a hair of your head will perish. 19By standing firm you
will gain life.

20"When you see Jerusalem being surrounded by armies, you
will know that its desolation is near. 21Then let those who are in
Judea flee to the mountains, let those in the city get out, and let
those in the country not enter the city. 22For this is the time of
punishment in fulfilment of all that has been written. 23How
dreadful it will be in those days for pregnant women and nursing
mothers! There will be great distress in the land and wrath against
this people. 24They will fall by the sword and will be taken as
prisoners to all the nations. Jerusalem will be trampled on by the
Gentiles until the times of the Gentiles are fulfilled.

25"There will be signs in the sun, moon and stars. On the earth,
nations will be in anguish and perplexity at the roaring and tossing
of the sea. 26Men will faint from terror, apprehensive of what is
coming on the world, for the heavenly bodies will be shaken. 27At
that time they will see the Son of Man coming in a cloud with
power and great glory. 28When these things begin to take place,
stand up and lift up your heads, because your redemption is
drawing near."

29He told them this parable: "Look at the fig-tree and all the
trees. 30When they sprout leaves, you can see for yourselves and
know that summer is near. 31Even so, when you see these things
happening, you know that the kingdom of God is near.

32"I tell you the truth, this generation will certainly not pass
away until all these things have happened. 33Heaven and earth
will pass away, but my words will never pass away.

34"Be careful, or your hearts will be weighed down with dissipa-
tion, drunkenness and the anxieties of life, and that day will close
on you unexpectedly like a trap. 35For it will come upon all those
who live on the face of the whole earth. 36Be always on the watch,
and pray that you may be able to escape all that is about to happen,
and that you may be able to stand before the Son of Man."

[37]Each day Jesus was teaching at the temple, and each evening
he went out to spend the night on the hill called the Mount of
Olives, [38]and all the people came early in the morning to hear him
at the temple.

Judas Agrees to Betray Jesus

22 Now the Feast of Unleavened Bread, called the Passover,
was approaching, [2]and the chief priests and the teachers of
the law were looking for some way to get rid of Jesus, for they were
afraid of the people. [3]Then Satan entered Judas, called Iscariot, one
of the Twelve. [4]And Judas went to the chief priests and the officers
of the temple guard and discussed with them how he might betray
Jesus. [5]They were delighted and agreed to give him money. [6]He
consented, and watched for an opportunity to hand Jesus over to
them when no crowd was present.

The Last Supper

[7]Then came the day of Unleavened Bread on which the Passover
lamb had to be sacrificed. [8]Jesus sent Peter and John, saying, "Go
and make preparations for us to eat the Passover."
[9]"Where do you want us to prepare for it?" they asked.
[10]He replied, "As you enter the city, a man carrying a jar of water
will meet you. Follow him to the house that he enters, [11]and say to
the owner of the house, 'The Teacher asks: Where is the guest
room, where I may eat the Passover with my disciples?' [12]He will
show you a large upper room, all furnished. Make preparations
there."
[13]They left and found things just as Jesus had told them. So they
prepared the Passover.
[14]When the hour came, Jesus and his apostles reclined at the
table. [15]And he said to them, "I have eagerly desired to eat this
Passover with you before I suffer. [16]For I tell you, I will not eat it
again until it finds fulfilment in the kingdom of God."
[17]After taking the cup, he gave thanks and said, "Take this and
divide it among you. [18]For I tell you I will not drink again of the
fruit of the vine until the kingdom of God comes."
[19]And he took bread, gave thanks and broke it, and gave it to

them, saying, "This is my body given for you; do this in remem-
brance of me."
[20]In the same way, after the supper he took the cup, saying,
"This cup is the new covenant in my blood, which is poured out for
you. [21]But the hand of him who is going to betray me is with mine
on the table. [22]The Son of Man will go as it has been decreed, but
woe to that man who betrays him." [23]They began to question
among themselves which of them it might be who would do this.
[24]Also a dispute arose among them as to which of them was
considered to be greatest. [25]Jesus said to them, "The kings of the
Gentiles lord it over them; and those who exercise authority over
them call themselves Benefactors. [26]But you are not to be like that.
Instead, the greatest among you should be like the youngest, and
the one who rules like the one who serves. [27]For who is greater,
the one who is at the table or the one who serves? Is it not the one
who is at the table? But I am among you as one who serves. [28]You
are those who have stood by me in my trials. [29]And I confer on you
a kingdom, just as my Father conferred one on me, [30]so that you
may eat and drink at my table in my kingdom and sit on thrones,
judging the twelve tribes of Israel.
[31]"Simon, Simon, Satan has asked to sift you as wheat. [32]But I
have prayed for you, Simon, that your faith may not fail. And
when you have turned back, strengthen your brothers."
[33]But he replied, "Lord, I am ready to go with you to prison and
to death."
[34]Jesus answered, "I tell you, Peter, before the cock crows today,
you will deny three times that you know me."
[35]Then Jesus asked them, "When I sent you without purse, bag
or sandals, did you lack anything?"
"Nothing," they answered.
[36]He said to them, "But now if you have a purse, take it, and also
a bag; and if you don't have a sword, sell your cloak and buy one.
[37]It is written: 'And he was numbered with the transgressors'; and
I tell you that this must be fulfilled in me. Yes, what is written
about me is reaching its fulfilment."
[38]The disciples said, "See, Lord, here are two swords."
"That is enough," he replied.

Jesus Prays on the Mount of Olives

[39]Jesus went out as usual to the Mount of Olives, and his

disciples followed him. [40]On reaching the place, he said to them,
"Pray that you will not fall into temptation." [41]He withdrew about

He knelt down and prayed (22:41)

a stone's throw beyond them, knelt down and prayed, [42]"Father, if
you are willing, take this cup from me; yet not my will, but yours
be done." [43]An angel from heaven appeared to him and strength-
ened him. [44]And being in anguish, he prayed more earnestly, and
his sweat was like drops of blood falling to the ground.
[45]When he rose from prayer and went back to the disciples, he
found them asleep, exhausted from sorrow. [46]"Why are you

sleeping?" he asked them. "Get up and pray so that you will not
fall into temptation."

Jesus Arrested

47While he was still speaking a crowd came up, and the man who
was called Judas, one of the Twelve, was leading them. He
approached Jesus to kiss him, 48but Jesus asked him, "Judas, are
you betraying the Son of Man with a kiss?"
49When Jesus' followers saw what was going to happen, they
said, "Lord, should we strike with our swords?" 50And one of
them struck the servant of the high priest, cutting off his right ear.
51But Jesus answered, "No more of this!" And he touched the
man's ear and healed him.
52Then Jesus said to the chief priests, the officers of the temple
guard, and the elders, who had come for him, "Am I leading a
rebellion, that you have come with swords and clubs? 53Every day I
was with you in the temple courts, and you did not lay a hand on
me. But this is your hour—when darkness reigns."

Peter Disowns Jesus

54Then seizing him, they led him away and took him into the
house of the high priest. Peter followed at a distance. 55But when
they had kindled a fire in the middle of the courtyard and had sat
down together, Peter sat down with them. 56A servant girl saw him
seated there in the firelight. She looked closely at him and said,
"This man was with him."
57But he denied it. "Woman, I don't know him," he said.
58A little later someone else saw him and said, "You also are one
of them."
"Man, I am not!" Peter replied.
59About an hour later another asserted, "Certainly this fellow
was with him, for he is a Galilean."
60Peter replied, "Man, I don't know what you're talking about!"
Just as he was speaking, the cock crowed. 61The Lord turned and
looked straight at Peter. Then Peter remembered the word the
Lord had spoken to him: "Before the cock crows today, you will
disown me three times." 62And he went outside and wept bitterly.

The Soldiers Mock Jesus

63The men who were guarding Jesus began mocking and beating
him. 64They blindfolded him and demanded, "Prophesy! Who hit
you?" 65And they said many other insulting things to him.

Jesus Before Pilate and Herod

66At daybreak the council of the elders of the people, both the
chief priests and teachers of the law, met together, and Jesus was
led before them. 67"If you are the Christ," they said, "tell us."

Jesus answered, "If I tell you, you will not believe me, 68and if I
asked you, you would not answer. 69But from now on, the Son of
Man will be seated at the right hand of the mighty God."

70They all asked, "Are you then the Son of God?"

He replied, "You are right in saying I am."

71Then they said, "Why do we need any more testimony? We
have heard it from his own lips."

23 Then the whole assembly rose and led him off to Pilate.
2And they began to accuse him, saying, "We have found
this man subverting our nation. He opposes payment of taxes to
Caesar and claims to be Christ, a king."

3So Pilate asked Jesus, "Are you the king of the Jews?"

"Yes, it is as you say," Jesus replied.

4Then Pilate announced to the chief priests and the crowd, "I
find no basis for a charge against this man."

5But they insisted, "He stirs up the people all over Judea by his
teaching. He started in Galilee and has come all the way here."

6On hearing this, Pilate asked if the man was a Galilean. 7When
he learned that Jesus was under Herod's jurisdiction, he sent him
to Herod, who was also in Jerusalem at that time.

8When Herod saw Jesus, he was greatly pleased, because for a
long time he had been wanting to see him. From what he had
heard about him, he hoped to see him perform some miracle. 9He
plied him with many questions, but Jesus gave him no answer.
10The chief priests and the teachers of the law were standing there,
vehemently accusing him. 11Then Herod and his soldiers ridiculed
and mocked him. Dressing him in an elegant robe, they sent him
back to Pilate. 12That day Herod and Pilate became friends—before
this they had been enemies.

13Pilate called together the chief priests, the rulers and the people, [14]and said to them, "You brought me this man as one who was inciting the people to rebellion. I have examined him in your presence and have found no basis for your charges against him. [15]Neither has Herod, for he sent him back to us; as you can see, he has done nothing to deserve death. [16]Therefore, I will punish him and then release him."

[18]With one voice they cried out, "Away with this man! Release Barabbas to us!" ([19]Barabbas had been thrown into prison for an insurrection in the city, and for murder.)

[20]Wanting to release Jesus, Pilate appealed to them again. [21]But they kept shouting, "Crucify him! Crucify him!"

[22]For the third time he spoke to them: "Why? What crime has this man committed? I have found in him no grounds for the death penalty. Therefore I will have him punished and then release him."

[23]But with loud shouts they insistently demanded that he be crucified, and their shouts prevailed. [24]So Pilate decided to grant their demand. [25]He released the man who had been thrown into prison for insurrection and murder, the one they asked for, and surrendered Jesus to their will.

The Crucifixion

[26]As they led him away, they seized Simon from Cyrene, who was on his way in from the country, and put the cross on him and made him carry it behind Jesus. [27]A large number of people followed him, including women who mourned and wailed for him. [28]Jesus turned and said to them, "Daughters of Jerusalem, do not weep for me; weep for yourselves and for your children. [29]For the time will come when you will say, 'Blessed are the barren women, the wombs that never bore and the breasts that never nursed!' [30]Then

"'they will say to the mountains, "Fall on us!"
and to the hills "Cover us!"'

[31]For if men do these things when the tree is green, what will happen when it is dry?"

[32]Two other men, both criminals, were also led out with him to be executed. [33]When they came to the place called the Skull, there

They crucified him, along with the criminals (23:33)

they crucified him, along with the criminals—one on his right, the
other on his left. 34Jesus said, "Father, forgive them, for they do
not know what they are doing." And they divided up his clothes
by casting lots.
35The people stood watching, and the rulers even sneered at
him. They said, "He saved others; let him save himself if he is the
Christ of God, the Chosen One."
36The soldiers also came up and mocked him. They offered him
wine vinegar 37and said, "If you are the king of the Jews, save
yourself."
38There was a written notice above him, which read: THIS IS THE
KING OF THE JEWS.
39One of the criminals who hung there hurled insults at him:
"Aren't you the Christ? Save yourself and us!"
40But the other criminal rebuked him. "Don't you fear God," he

said, "since you are under the same sentence? 41We are punished
justly, for we are getting what our deeds deserve. But this man has
done nothing wrong."
42Then he said, "Jesus, remember me when you come into your
kingdom."
43Jesus answered him, "I tell you the truth, today you will be
with me in paradise."

Jesus' Death

44It was now about the sixth hour, and darkness came over the
whole land until the ninth hour, 45for the sun stopped shining.
And the curtain of the temple was torn in two. 46Jesus called out
with a loud voice, "Father, into your hands I commit my spirit."
When he had said this, he breathed his last.
47The centurion, seeing what had happened, praised God and
said, "Surely this was a righteous man." 48When all the people
who had gathered to witness this sight saw what took place, they
beat their breasts and went away. 49But all those who knew him,
including the women who had followed him from Galilee, stood at
a distance, watching these things.

Jesus' Burial

50Now there was a man named Joseph, a member of the Council,
a good and upright man, 51who had not consented to their decision
and action. He came from the Judean town of Arimathea and he
was waiting for the kingdom of God. 52Going to Pilate, he asked for
Jesus' body. 53Then he took it down, wrapped it in linen cloth and
placed it in a tomb cut in the rock, one in which no-one had yet
been laid. 54It was Preparation Day, and the Sabbath was about to
begin.
55The women who had come with Jesus from Galilee followed
Joseph and saw the tomb and how his body was laid in it. 56Then
they went home and prepared spices and perfumes. But they
rested on the Sabbath in obedience to the commandment.

The Resurrection

24 On the first day of the week, very early in the morning, the
women took the spices they had prepared and went to the
tomb. 2They found the stone rolled away from the tomb, 3but

when they entered, they did not find the body of the Lord Jesus. 4While they were wondering about this, suddenly two men in clothes that gleamed like lightning stood beside them. 5In their fright the women bowed down with their faces to the ground, but the men said to them, "Why do you look for the living among the

He is not here; he has risen! (24:6)

dead? 6He is not here; he has risen! Remember how he told you, while he was still with you in Galilee: 7'The Son of Man must be delivered into the hands of sinful men, be crucified and on the third day be raised again.'" 8Then they remembered his words.

9When they came back from the tomb, they told all these things to the Eleven and to all the others. 10It was Mary Magdalene, Joanna, Mary the mother of James, and the others with them who told this to the apostles. 11But they did not believe the women, because their words seemed to them like nonsense. 12Peter, however, got up and ran to the tomb. Bending over, he saw the strips of linen lying by themselves, and he went away, wondering to himself what had happened.

On the Road to Emmaus

[13]Now that same day two of them were going to a village called
Emmaus, about seven miles from Jerusalem. [14]They were talking
with each other about everything that had happened. [15]As they
talked and discussed these things with each other, Jesus himself
came up and walked along with them; [16]but they were kept from
recognising him.

[17]He asked them, "What are you discussing together as you
walk along?"

They stood still, their faces downcast. [18]One of them, named
Cleopas, asked him, "Are you only a visitor to Jerusalem and do
not know the things that have happened there in these days?"

[19]"What things?" he asked.

"About Jesus of Nazareth," they replied. "He was a prophet,
powerful in word and deed before God and all the people. [20]The
chief priests and our rulers handed him over to be sentenced to
death, and they crucified him; [21]but we had hoped that he was the
one who was going to redeem Israel. And what is more, it is the
third day since all this took place. [22]In addition, some of our
women amazed us. They went to the tomb early this morning [23]but
didn't find his body. They came and told us that they had seen a
vision of angels, who said he was alive. [24]Then some of our
companions went to the tomb and found it just as the women had
said, but him they did not see."

[25]He said to them, "How foolish you are, and how slow of heart
to believe all that the prophets have spoken! [26]Did not the Christ
have to suffer these things and then enter his glory?" [27]And
beginning with Moses and all the Prophets, he explained to them
what was said in all the Scriptures concerning himself.

[28]As they approached the village to which they were going,
Jesus acted as if he were going further. [29]But they urged him
strongly, "Stay with us, for it is nearly evening; the day is almost
over." So he went in to stay with them.

[30]When he was at the table with them, he took bread, gave
thanks, broke it and began to give it to them. [31]Then their eyes
were opened and they recognised him, and he disappeared from
their sight. [32]They asked each other, "Were not our hearts burning
within us while he talked with us on the road and opened the
Scriptures to us?"

[33]They got up and returned at once to Jerusalem. There they
found the Eleven and those with them, assembled together [34]and

saying, "It is true! The Lord has risen and has appeared to Simon."
35Then the two told what had happened on the way, and how
Jesus was recognised by them when he broke the bread.

Jesus Appears to the Disciples

36While they were still talking about this, Jesus himself stood
among them and said to them, "Peace be with you."
37They were startled and frightened, thinking they saw a ghost.
38He said to them, "Why are you troubled, and why do doubts rise
in your minds? 39Look at my hands and my feet. It is I myself!
Touch me and see; a ghost does not have flesh and bones, as you
see I have."
40When he had said this, he showed them his hands and feet.
41And while they still did not believe it because of joy and amaze-
ment, he asked them, "Do you have anything here to eat?" 42They
gave him a piece of broiled fish, 43and he took it and ate it in their
presence.
44He said to them, "This is what I told you while I was still with
you: Everything must be fulfilled that is written about me in the
Law of Moses, the Prophets and the Psalms."
45Then he opened their minds so they could understand the
Scriptures. 46He told them, "This is what is written: The Christ will
suffer and rise from the dead on the third day, 47and repentance
and forgiveness of sins will be preached in his name to all nations,
beginning at Jerusalem. 48You are witnesses of these things. 49I am
going to send you what my Father has promised; but stay in the
city until you have been clothed with power from on high."

The Ascension

50When he had led them out to the vicinity of Bethany, he lifted
up his hands and blessed them. 51While he was blessing them, he
left them and was taken up into heaven. 52Then they worshipped
him and returned to Jerusalem with great joy. 53And they stayed
continually at the temple, praising God.

WORD LIST

Please note that the italicised words are explained under a separate entry in the Word List.

Abel The second son of Adam and Eve, murdered by his elder brother Cain.
Abraham The founder of the Hebrew people.
Abyss (8:31) The Jews believed this to be deep in the earth where demons were imprisoned until their final and complete destruction.
Alabaster A soft stone from which pots, vases and jars were made.
Angel Heavenly messenger and servant of God.
Apostle One of the twelve disciples of Jesus. Later it referred to Paul and Luke and other Christian leaders. The word means "one who is sent".

Baptism It comes from the word which means to dip or immerse. When a person is baptised, he is dipped in water or has water sprinkled on him as an outward sign that he is truly sorry for his sins and turns to God. Jesus was baptised to show his oneness with us.
Beelzebub Another name for the *Devil* or Satan.
Blasphemy Against the *Holy Spirit* (12:10). Attributing to the Devil something that clearly is of God.

Caesar The Emperor of Rome.
Capstone The top or finishing stone of a building.
Centurion A Roman officer in charge of a hundred men.
Christ The anointed or promised one. Jesus was called Christ, because God chose him and sent him to save us from our sins.
Circumcise To cut off the foreskin of the penis. It was the sign of God's *covenant* with his people Israel. This was done to the Jewish boys eight days after birth.
Consolation of Israel (2:25) This refers to the promised Messiah or Christ or Deliverer of the Jewish people.

Covenant An agreement between people, or between God and a person or group of people.
Cross A Roman method of execution. The victim was nailed to a cross of wood through his hands and feet and left to die in great pain and shame.
Curtain of the Temple (23:45) This huge curtain divided the outer Court of the *Temple* from the Holiest of All. Only the High Priest was allowed in this and then only once a year on the Day of Atonement. Jesus' death opened up the way right into God's presence.

Demon An evil spirit.
Denarius A coin worth about 50p.
Devil A name for the chief demon or evil spirit.
Disciple A learner or a follower. It is used by Luke for the followers of first John the Baptist and then Jesus.

Elijah A great Old Testament prophet. He defeated the prophets of the god Baal on Mount Carmel.
Elisha He was Elijah's assistant and took over as the leading prophet when Elijah was taken to Heaven.

Faith Personal trust in God.
Fasting Going without food in order to pray or as a religious duty.

Heaven The eternal home of God and of all his believing people after this life.
Hell (Hades) The name for the world of torment inhabited by the unbelieving dead, in contrast to Heaven.
Herod The King or ruler of the Jews. Under the Romans he had very little actual power.
Holy Spirit The Spirit of God at work in the world.
Hypocrisy Play-acting, pretending to be what you are not.

Isaiah One of the most famous of the Old Testament prophets. He lived in the eighth century before Christ. He wrote in detail about the suffering the Christ would go through to save his people.

Jacob The grandson of Abraham. He was later given the name of Israel.

Jerusalem The chief city of Israel and the centre of worship.
Jesus The name means Saviour or Rescuer.
Jonah The Hebrew prophet who was rescued after being swallowed by a huge fish and so enabled to carry out God's orders to preach in Nineveh, the capital of Assyria.

Kingdom of God Where God rules and especially in the hearts of his people.
Korazin A town on the sea of Galilee.

Law Usually this refers to the first five books of the Old Testament, sometimes to the Ten Commandments given to Moses.
Leprosy A fatal skin disease very common in the Middle East and Africa. The word used in the Bible can refer to other skin diseases.
Levite A member of the Israelite tribe of Levi. His special task was to help in the *Temple* worship.

Mina A coin worth about three months' wages.
Miracle An act of supernatural power not possible by ordinary means.
Moses The man chosen by God to lead the Hebrew people out of slavery in Egypt. God gave him the *Law* or commandments for the people to obey.

Naaman A Syrian general who was healed of leprosy by the ninth-century B.C. prophet Elisha.

Parable A story that makes a point of great meaning.
Paradise Another name for *Heaven*.
Passover A major Jewish festival.
Pharisee A strict Jewish religious party whose aim was to keep the *Law* in the tiniest detail.
Prophet Someone who proclaims God's message.
Purification After childbirth a woman was considered unclean until she had come to the *Temple* and offered either a lamb or two doves or pigeons as a sacrifice.

Queen of the South The Queen of Sheba, probably the present Yemen, who came to visit King Solomon.

Redemption Another word for *salvation*.
Repentance A turning from sin and turning to God.

Resurrection 1. God the Father raising Jesus from the dead. 2. Because of Jesus' resurrection God will raise all his believing people from death to eternal life with him in *Heaven*.

Sabbath The seventh day of the Jewish week, set apart for worship, when no work of any kind was to be done.
Sacrifice An act of worship by which an offering was made to God of something belonging to the person.
Salvation In the New Testament it means being rescued from the power and consequences of sin by the death of Jesus on the Cross.
Samaria The region between Judea and Galilee. Because of differences especially in religion the Jews and Samaritans hated each other.
Sanctuary A building or part of a building for the worship of God.
Satan Another name for the *Devil*.
Sidon An ancient city in the present Lebanon, burnt to the ground in about the year 350 B.C.
Sodom A wicked city destroyed by God in the time of *Abraham*.
Son of Man A title used by Jesus which is found in the Book of Daniel to describe the coming Messiah.
Synagogue A meeting place for worship, hearing the Law of God and for the governing of the civil life of the community.

Tax collectors The Romans occupied the land of Israel. They appointed Jewish tax collectors to collect revenue. The Jews hated and despised them and saw them as traitors.
Temple The building in Jerusalem that was the centre of Jewish worship.
Tetrarch Herod the Great divided his Kingdom into four sections for his four sons to rule. Each was called the tetrarch and the word means "ruler of a fourth part".
Theophilus Luke dedicates his two books to Theophilus. It is not certain whether this was the real name of a well-known noble or just a general word for the Christian reader. The word means "friend of God".
Tyre An important sea port to the north-west of Galilee.

Zechariah 1. The father of John the Baptist. 2. In 11:51 this probably refers to the sixth-century *prophet* who was martyred for his obedience to God's word (see 2 Chronicles 24:20–22).

WHAT TO DO NOW

You have just been reading the Gospel of Luke. Almost certainly you did this by yourself – it isn't easy for more than one person to read a book at the same time!

But Christians are not meant to be Christians by themselves nor are they meant to keep their Christianity to themselves.

Here are four things every new Christian should do:

1 Join a church. A church is far more than a building. It is the people who meet in the building. Jesus wanted us to realise that as God is our Father, we are all brothers and sisters. The Church is the family of God. (The people who gave you this book can advise you on what church to join if you don't know where to look.)
It is often difficult to join a new group of people and no church is perfect, but do it and you will be glad that you made the effort!

2 Start reading the Bible. Luke is only one part of the Bible. Some of the other books are more difficult to grasp at first reading. Ask the minister at the church you join for advice about the various systems and booklets that are available to help you understand the Bible. Most churches have Bible study groups. Ask about joining one.

3 Make a time every day when you can be alone with God and pray. Look at page 50 and think about Jesus' teaching on prayer. You don't need any special language. God loves you and wants to hear what is on your heart.

4 Start sharing what you have found out about Jesus Christ with other people you know. That is why Luke wrote his Gospel. God does not ask you to 'preach at' people or to claim to be better than others. He simply asks you to show his love to others and to give them a chance to discover what Jesus Christ has done for the world.

This copy of the Gospel of Luke is a small part of the whole Bible. It is vital for every new Christian to become familiar with the complete text of the Bible in the course of time. To assist individuals and groups who have become Christians through the 'Billy Graham Mission 89', copies of the complete New Testament in the New International Version are available on request. These New Testaments are available for personal use and are not for resale. Please complete and post the coupon to Scripture Gift Mission at the address below before 30th September 1989.

To: **SCRIPTURE GIFT MISSION**
Radstock House
3 Eccleston Street
LONDON SW1W 9LZ

Please send my personal copy of the New Testament (NIV).

Name ....

Address ....

....

THE NEW INTERNATIONAL VERSION

The New International Version is a modern English translation acclaimed for its accurate scholarship, its lucid, dignified English, and the clarity with which it communicates the timeless truths of Scripture.

More than one hundred scholars from diverse denominational backgrounds worked for fifteen years to complete this distinctive translation. Their overruling concern was to be faithful to the text of Scripture, and faithfully to reflect the literary and stylistic diversity within the Bible. The result is a Bible eminently suitable both for private study and public reading.